Client-Centered Service: How to Keep Them Coming Back for More

David W. Cottle

WILEY

John Wiley & Sons

New York • Chichester • Brisbane • Toronto • SIngapore

Library of Congress Cataloging-in-Publication Data

Cottle, David W.
    Client-centered service: how to keep them coming back for more /
David W. Cottle.
        p.   cm.
    Includes bibliographical references.
    ISBN 0-471-50969-8
    1. Customer service.   2. Professions—Marketing.   3. Customer
satisfaction.   4. Quality control.   I. Title.
HF5415.5.C68   1989
658.8'12—dc20   89-22426
                                                                          CIP

Printed in the United States of America

10 9 8 7 6 5 4 3 2 1

Those three facts, taken together, mean that marketing power shifts from your generic service to other ways in which prospects can clearly perceive differences between your firm and your competitors.

It's not easy to be distinctive because professional services are actually doubly intangible. First, the service itself is intangible, just like any other service. Second, because professional services require long years of specialized study and practice, they are difficult for clients to grasp mentally. Therefore, professional services are also mentally intangible. This double intangibility makes all your internal distinctions and technical superiority invisible to your market. Therefore, you have to concentrate on standing above the crowd by presenting your firm as unique in ways your clients *can* perceive.

Key Point: You cannot achieve uniqueness in your basic, generic service.

If you cannot stand above the crowd through the internal quality of your basic output, how can you be unique?

Recall that people buy your services for only two reasons: to solve their problems or to get good feelings. Clients value your service in direct proportion to its perceived ability to solve their problems or make them feel good. So your service is a complex cluster of values that are unique to each client because each client's viewpoint is unique.

But most clients expect more than just basic services.

Examples:

- A real estate broker's refusal to return phone calls may cause sellers and other brokers to refuse to deal with him or her.

- A stock broker's confusing monthly statements may drive investors away.

- A doctor's habit of making patients cool their heels for an hour in the waiting room may cause them not to return.

- Any professional may have scored very high on his or her licensing examination, but an abrasive personality may send potential clients elsewhere.

As we have seen, the key to client satisfaction is to give them more than they expect, or more than they are accustomed to getting elsewhere, or, as Tom Peters says, "Underpromise and overdeliver!" To do this, you need to find ways to augment your basic service with extras. Most of these extras must come in the area of external quality, because that is most visible to clients.

The good news is that external quality is much easier and cheaper to improve than internal quality.

Examples:

- A stock brokerage firm includes with customers' monthly statements a current balance sheet for each customer and a source- and application-of-funds statement.

- A CPA firm sends its clients an automobile log at year end so they can substantiate their mileage deductions more easily.

- A law firm offers to send copies of a client's will to his or her children, CPA, and insurance agent.

- A surgeon sends patients flowers for their hospital rooms.

- A doctor who gets behind schedule in the morning has the nurse call patients with afternoon appointments to have them delay their arrivals.

Caution: Client expectations are progressive. As Theodore Levitt[5] points out, over time, providing these extras will educate your clients about what is reasonable to expect from your firm. Eventually, competitors begin to offer these extras and, soon, they are no longer extra, they are part of clients' expectations. Client expectations rise to what has been shown to be possible.

Example: Remember when only the "best" hotels provided personal sized shampoo bottles in their guest rooms? Now most hotels do it.

The more successfully you expand your market by giving clients more and better quality service and raising their expectations, the more vulnerable you become to losing those clients. That's just the way it is.

Questions To Think About:

- How are your services different from your competitors'?

- What characteristics distinguish your firm from your competition?

- How can you further differentiate your services?

THOSE LITTLE EXTRAS

To set yourself apart from your competition, look for differentiation factors and unique characteristics. True differentiation seldom comes from a single "big-bang" advantage. As mentioned earlier, differentiation involves not one thing done 100 percent better than anyone else; it involves 10 things done 10 percent better. Or even 100 things done 1 percent better. That's why it is so hard to do—and to beat.

Use "creative swiping." Look at what other firms both in your profession and in others are doing, and ask yourself if you can adapt those features to your practice.

Examples:

- Many practice procedures of accountants and some types of lawyers are very similar. A business-oriented CPA practice serves the same type of clients as a corporate law firm. A heavily income-tax-oriented CPA practice, on the other hand, might serve the same types of clients as a personal injury lawyer or a family law practice.

- Many medical practitioners' practices are quite similar. Physicians could learn from dentists and vice versa. Chiropractors and family practitioners could get ideas from each other.

- Architects, engineers, and planners have very similar practices.

And don't think that just because you are a professional, you can't—or shouldn't—learn something from a well-run business.

Examples:

- Dave Reznick (a founding partner of Reznick Fedder & Silverman in Bethesda, Maryland) got the idea for using "The Ten Commandments of Good Business" in his practice from seeing it hanging on the wall of one of his clients.

- I first noticed the value of a good telephone receptionist from a Dallas savings and loan association.

Any place you see superior customer service—whether in a restaurant or a dry cleaner—ask yourself, "How can I adapt what they're doing to my practice so that I can serve my clients better?"

One experienced professional with a good record of client referrals explains, "The formula for getting referrals from clients is *caring*. Caring is thoughtfulness for another's welfare, well-being or success and, sometimes, an almost hovering attentiveness to the other's concerns or problems." If this sounds familiar, it's because the professional is talking about the quality dimensions of assurance and empathy. Or, as L. Ron Hubbard[6] said: "The essence of good management is CARING what goes on" (all-capitals emphasis in original).

Caring involves extraordinary attention to opportunities to go the extra mile, such as

- A voluntary fee reduction because of unexpected efficiency

- Writing a letter at the conclusion of the service with helpful suggestions for improving the client's operations

- Paying goodwill visits to clients throughout the year without charging them for the time

- Clipping newspaper or magazine articles about things that you know are of interest to particular clients and sending them a copy with a personal note

- Remembering birthdays or anniversaries of important events to clients or clients' businesses, such as the founding of the business or the opening of its first branch or other milestones in the development of the business

Caring does take time, but it doesn't have to cost much money. Also, you can use assistants' time to do some items. Mainly, caring just takes adopting a mind-set of focusing your attention on your clients and continually asking yourself what more you can do for them.

PERCEPTION IS REALITY AND FEELINGS ARE FACTS

This is so important that I will repeat it:

> **Definition:** *Reality* is what you can perceive clearly.

Have you ever looked through a thick fog at a distant building? You couldn't make it out very well; it looked sort of unreal. In fact, it might have been a mountain, or a billboard; you just couldn't tell. For something to be real to you, you must not only perceive it; you must perceive it clearly. Because people cannot clearly perceive your technical expertise, they must rely on other things to indicate your competence.

The key factor in client satisfaction is not how good you are at your profession, but how you are perceived by your clients—in other words, your image. And the key factor in marketing success is not how good you are at your profession, but how good you are perceived to be by prospects and referral sources. Good marketing causes a client or referral source to think of you when they have the opportunity to recommend a professional.

The key factors in determining your image are the perception principles.

> **Key Point—Perception Principle Number Four:** People will perceive that your performance in nonbusiness settings is an indication of your performance in your profession.[7]

In other words, if you cheat on the golf course, your golf partners will suspect that you approach your professional responsibilities the same way. People use your performance as a tennis player, parent, Little League coach, etc. as a surrogate of your performance as a professional. They may not know how you will handle yourself under pressure professionally, but they can sure tell how you handle yourself in the last quarter of a schoolboy football game when your team is down six points.

> **Key Point—Perception Principle Number Five:** People will also perceive that your performance in one area of your business is representative of your performance in *all other* areas of your business.

Your clients may not be able to tell how well you do research, but they can clearly perceive whether your library is neat. They may not know whether you are up on the latest developments in your specialty, but they do know whether your receptionist knows how to pronounce their name. They may not know how well you performed the service, but they know what your souvenirs (documents and other deliverables) look like.

These perception principles hold because clients have no means to judge your internal quality or competence, so by default, they fall back on those things they do feel competent to grade you on. Their evaluation of your performance in these nontechnical areas (external quality, nonbusiness performance, souvenirs, and performance in areas of your business they feel qualified to judge) serves as a surrogate for your technical performance. Then their evaluation of these nontechnical areas carries over to your technical performance.

This principle of transference works for companies, as well as for individuals. The positive effects of these "rub-off" perceptions can be as beneficial as the negative effects are detrimental. Thus, many fine companies like to be identified with sponsoring public television programs and visible corporate citizenship programs locally.

This is important because perception is all there is. There is no *reality* as such. Reality to you is only what you perceive. And what you perceive is your reality. Clients are no different. To them, feelings *are* facts.

To illustrate the fourth perception principle in action, consider the abrupt resignation of a prominent senator from the 1988 Democratic presidential nomination campaign on the disclosure of his involvement with a woman who was not his wife.

A good example of the fifth perception principle is another senator's departure from the 1988 Democratic presidential nomination race when it was disclosed that some of his best speeches were plagiarized from other politicians, as well as at least one of his college papers. The public perceived that his lack of integrity in one area of his career spoke badly of his professional competence in other areas.

Just so you won't think I'm picking on Democrats, recall that one of

President Reagan's nominations to the Supreme Court was withdrawn after charges surfaced that the nominated judge had smoked marijuana while holding a Justice Department position. This violated both the fourth and the fifth perception principles.

As Don Burr, then-chairman of People Express, noted, "Coffee stains on the flip-down trays [in our airplanes] mean [to the passengers] that we do our engine maintenance wrong." Likewise, a telephone operator in your firm who garbles your client's message means to clients that you are also screwing up your service to them.

However, there can also be positive effects of these two phenomena. In fact, the positive effects of these "rub-off" perceptions can be as beneficial as the negative effects are detrimental. Thus, many companies like to be identified as sponsoring public television programs and visible corporate citizenship programs locally. If you become membership chairperson of a club or organization and do a superlative job, or if you become a fund-raising chairman whose target is $50,000 and you raise $100,000, people will also think well of your professional abilities.

Questions To Think About:

- Look at your own buying habits with respect to a doctor, an airline, an accountant, a stock broker, a banker, a plumber. Why do you sustain a relationship?

- Look at several business relationships you have severed. Why did you do it?

- How did you choose a new supplier? What are the perceptual attributes of your decision to buy or sustain or leave?

The subjects of image and perception are so important that the entire next chapter is devoted to them.

NOTES

1. Thomas J. Peters and Nancy Austin, *A Passion for Excellence*, New York: Warner Books, 1985, p. 71.
2. Theodore Levitt, *The Marketing Imagination*, New York: The Free Press, 1986, p. 73.

3.   Theodore Levitt, p. 72.

4.   Theodore Levitt, pp. 78–79.

5.   Theodore Levitt, p. 82.

6.   L. Ron Hubbard, *Management Series Volume 2*, Los Angeles: Bridge Publications, 1983, p. 16.

7.   Mike McCaffrey called this "the Transfer Rule," *Personal Marketing Strategies*, Englewood Cliffs, NJ: Prentice-Hall, 1983.

9

How to Project a
High-Quality Image

Definition: *Image* is a likeness or imitation of a person or thing—
a mental picture or conception.

It is perfectly clear that your image is not you. In fact, you could have
an image that bears little or no resemblance to the real you. Your firm
could also have an image that does not present an accurate representation of the caliber of service you render. In other words, your image
might have little relationship to what you consider reality.

Then why care what your image is? Because perception is reality.
Your clients' and prospects' perceptions or opinions about you and
your firm determine their reality about you. When someone looks at
you, what do they see? You might think they see you, but actually only
about 5 percent of what they see is you; the rest is your appearance,
including your clothes and haircut or hairdo! The overall effect they
see creates a mental picture or conception that gives the viewer some
clues as to what sort of professional you might be. For those who don't
know you, that image, and what you might say to them, is all the
information they have with which to judge you. To them, that image *is*
the *real* you.

People get one message if you are wearing business attire, but they get a different message if you are wearing sports clothes. Your business suit, your tie or scarf, and your shirt or blouse give them tangible clues as to who you are. These things can say, among other things, "This person means business," or "This person doesn't care."

How would they react if you were dressed for business otherwise, but you were wearing running shoes? They would probably be confused. To avoid confusing your clients or sending mixed messages, dress consistently. Create a commanding, confident image with consistent messages.

The same applies to your firm. Everyone in your firm should project a high-quality image because the combined image created by your firm's personnel gives the public clues as to what sort of firm you are. And for those who don't know any different, your image is all the information they have to judge whether they want to talk to you about their professional needs.

If someone ever gets to know you or your firm, they will certainly have a more accurate picture of the person you are and the firm you represent both professionally and personally. However, if you and your firm don't make the right impression on others, you'll never get the chance! In other words, if you don't develop a positive, professional image of yourself and your firm in the minds of clients, potential clients, and referral sources, the odds are you will not get those referrals, nor will your clients recommend you to others.

Though the cliché may seem unfair, it is true: *You never get a second chance to make a first impression.* When asked to recommend a firm, what image first comes to clients' and prospects' minds when your name is mentioned?

Many more people know *of* you than are personally acquainted with you. And many more people are only acquainted with you than really know you. The funny thing is, all those people—regardless of how well they know you—have an image of you. It is the mental picture they get when your name is mentioned. The better they know you, the more accurate their mental picture will be.

But the converse is also true. The less they know you, the less real, first-hand information they have on what kind of person you are, and what kind of firm you represent.

Well, then, how do people form their mental picture? What information goes into their minds to make up the picture? Your image has two parts: your personal image and the image of your firm. Images are formed by a series of impressions people gain. This is true for both your personal and your firm's images.

YOUR PERSONAL IMAGE

Personal impressions are composed largely of appearance, communication, and actions.

Appearance

Appearance is just that—what you look like. It includes your clothes, your grooming, and your posture and gestures. Yes, "Appearances can be deceiving," and, "You can't tell a book by its cover." Nonetheless, book publishers spend millions of dollars on research each year to discover which subtle clues on the covers help to sell their books.

> **Example:** Did you ever notice a bookstore display of the same book in which half the books had red covers and half had blue covers? Everything else about the covers was identical except the colors. Or perhaps the colors were the same but the typeface in which the book title was set was different. That was a market test. The publisher was testing to discover what subtle difference color or type style would have on book sales.

These savvy businesspeople realize—for good or bad, rightly or wrongly—the cover has an influence on selling the book.

Similarly, your personal appearance sends definite messages—messages that sometimes neither the sender nor the receiver are aware of. Whether you like it or not, it is a fact that people are influenced by your appearance.

Because people are going to be influenced by your appearance, which way do you want them to be influenced? Do you want your appearance to speak as well of you as you deserve? Or do you want your appearance to speak worse of you than you really are?

Remember, 95 percent of what people see of you is only your clothes and your hairstyle.

Questions To Think About:

- What kind of message does your clothing send?
- What message does your hairstyle send?
- What do they say about you?

The bottom line is that the way you dress affects the way you are perceived by others. Either dress so that people don't notice what you are wearing, or dress so that your attire makes a positive statement. Generally, it is better to be more conservative than less. It is better to look richer than poorer. It is better to be understated than overstated.

Key Point: Clothes help make the sale.

Communication

Communicate in ways that reinforce your image of high quality, including

- Your voice
- The words you use
- The jokes you tell
- The subjects you discuss

Communication also overlaps with appearance to include your body language—the way you walk, carry yourself, and make gestures.

People's number-one fear—even more feared than death—is fear of speaking before a group. Even if you never make a speech, the way you speak one-on-one or in social groups has a profound effect on your image. Effective speaking will not automatically stand you apart from the crowd, but ineffective speaking can almost surely guarantee you will remain anonymous—or notorious. The offensive word, the poor choice of words, the angry word—once spoken, these cannot be recalled. The boring tone, the unpleasant voice, the unpleasant personal mannerism are all to be avoided.

Numerous cassette programs are available to help you improve your ability to speak in public. Also, Bert Decker[1] has suggested that if you think you don't speak in public, think again. You certainly don't speak in private! Anytime you are talking to someone other than yourself you are speaking in public. Buy one of these programs and listen to it several times and practice, practice, practice. It will help you communicate a high-quality image.

Don't use profanity, even if you hear the client or prospect use it. Why take a chance on offending someone else within earshot? Also, it does not speak well for your professional image, even to someone who is profane.

Humor (such as teasing or jokes) also can be dangerous unless you are good at it. Avoid long stories or jokes in poor taste (e.g., morbid, ethnic, or vulgar jokes). Also, sarcasm can turn people off very quickly—especially people who don't know you well.

Actions

High-quality actions speak louder than any words. Action can demonstrate your competence and the quality of your service far better than words can. Actions include your personal, business, civic, and charitable activities, as well as the professional experiences people have had with you. I repeat the fourth and fifth perception principles here, to emphasize their importance in clients' and prospects' perceptions of your actions:

- People will perceive that your performance in nonbusiness settings is an indication of your performance in your profession.

- People will perceive that your competence in one area of your practice is representative of your performance in all other areas of your practice.

Apply the perception principles to your discretionary, nonprofessional activities: To be perceived favorably by others, be active, be effective, and be visible.

Be Active

To help you to be active, select a project or organization that you enjoy. This is gratifying to you whether or not it helps your business and gives you a good feeling about how you are spending your discretionary time. This in turn makes it easier to stay active.

You can find openings for constructive actions in civic, social, charitable, and even political organizations. Civic and charitable activities, such as school-, church-, and symphony-related activities have an added advantage that social clubs do not: the bonding that occurs when dedicated people work together toward a worthwhile common goal.

Activity	More fertile	Less fertile
Tennis	Country club	Local public tennis courts
Education	School board	PTA
Business	Chamber of Commerce	Jaycees
Fitness	Athletic club	YMCA gym
Culture	Friends of the Opera	Square dance club
Charity	Church auction	Food for the poor

Table 1
Fertile and Infertile Areas for Making Contacts

Be Effective

Clearly, you only involve yourself in activities in which you can be effective. Don't overextend yourself to the point of being ineffective, and don't choose activities in which you can't competently follow through on your tasks. The way you perform here will indicate to others how well you perform as a professional.

Be Visible

Your involvement and activism will demonstrate your leadership qualities only if you are also visible. So choose your arena with care. You can labor long and diligently as treasurer of the Opera Guild, but you won't get as much visibility as the fund-raising chairperson. You can work hard at the Kiwanis hot-dog stand at the local arts festival, but you won't be noticed as much as the membership chairperson.

One other thing, plant your seeds in *fertile ground*—any area that could lead to business opportunities later on. Table 1 gives some examples. The point of your action is to expend your efforts where you can make contacts and develop relationships with the largest number of prospective clients and referral sources. In other words, "Hunt where the ducks are!"

YOUR FIRM'S IMAGE

Clients' and prospects' impressions of a firm are composed of

- Combined impressions of the firm's personnel, particularly the frontline personnel

- The appearance of documents, reports, correspondence, newsletters, and other tangible products the client receives from the firm

- Office facilities and equipment

Your Personnel

A firm is nothing more than a group of individuals. To a certain extent, the firm's image is also the image of the group of individuals who make up the firm. But it is more. The images of individuals in the firm tend to reinforce one another, particularly if they are bad images. If you know ten individuals in the same firm, and one is slovenly while nine are well dressed, you may think the one is an oddball who will not be around long. But if you know two who are slovenly, then you think there is something wrong with the firm.

One or two bad impressions of your firm can ruin a whole string of good impressions. So everything I said about good personal impressions goes double if you are part of a firm. Therefore, if you are serious about your business, you want that attitude projected to your clients by your personnel. Proper business attire says that you mean business. Clothes should not distract people. Men and women who represent you should wear clothes that say, "I mean business." You might be surprised to know that IBM has no written policy that tells employees how to dress; that's a fact, according to Buck Rogers,[2] IBM's recently retired national Marketing Vice President. And he ought to know. But to be completely truthful, Buck says that there is an unwritten dress code as effective as if it were engraved in steel.

So the honest answer to the question, "Does IBM require its employees to wear white shirts and quiet ties?" is, "Yes."

Here's why: In all kinds of businesses, people work in uniforms, and no one thinks anything about it. The uniform is usually designed to help the person who wears it perform the job as efficiently as possible. Have you ever played tennis or golf with a person who was "out of uniform" or wearing attire that was inappropriate for tennis or golf? Weren't you distracted?

"That's one of the points of IBM's unwritten dress code. Clothes should not . . . distract people. Men and women who are on the job representing IBM wear business suits. That's because IBM is serious about its business and wants its attitude projected to its customers by its front people."

What do you do about the staff or partner who dresses inappropriately? For staff people, get them a copy of a book on business attire; there are several good ones for both men and women. For partners, it is a matter of personal counseling from the managing partner.

Your Key Salesperson

Who in your firm has the most moments of truth with clients, prospects, and referral sources? The telephone operator. In most firms, the receptionist and telephone operator are the same person. Frequently, the receptionist is the lowest-paid, least-trained, least-experienced, and least-respected person in the firm. If this is true of your firm, your firm is missing a bet because receptionists can be key players in presenting a high-quality image to the public. I recommend that your receptionist be your highest-paid support person except for your firm administrator.

You might think a client's or prospect's first meeting is with the partner in charge of the relationship or the one who made the contact. Actually, most people who enter your office have their first moment of truth with your receptionist. He or she can be your best salesperson.

Give your receptionist the name of everyone you are expecting. Allow your receptionist to greet visitors by name and to make them feel comfortable if the person they came to see is not immediately available when they arrive. Remember that your receptionist will be prospects' most frequent contact if they become clients. Make sure those introductions get off on the right foot.

Have your receptionist offer every visitor some refreshment. Even if you will come to collect the visitor immediately, the offer shows good manners. Visitors may be carrying briefcases or coats. Your receptionist should offer to hang coats in your coat closet. Visitors will want to retain briefcases.

If visitors have not finished their refreshments when you arrive, your receptionist should *volunteer* to take either the refreshments or the briefcase, or both to your desk. This is especially important with prospects to whom you give an office tour first, because they can't very well carry full cups of coffee or other beverage, as well as briefcases, around the office. Even if they could, they could not then shake hands with the key people to whom you will introduce them.

Meet each visitor personally in the reception area; don't send a secretary to fetch your guest. If your visitor will be seeing more than one person in your office, each person should personally take the visitor to the next person and introduce the visitor.

> **Key Point:** After the appearance of your reception area, the next most powerful image prospects will get of your firm is how they are greeted and treated when they enter your offices.

By paying proper attention to the many facets of your image, you can send the right messages to your clients and prospects.

Your Tangible Products

Your Ambassadors

You have lots of "ambassadors" representing you when you aren't around. I'm not just talking about the other people in your firm. Your client newsletters, brochures, announcements, business cards, and so forth are ambassadors representing you when you aren't there. Once you think about it, that's why they are there, isn't it? To represent your firm when you're not there and to keep reminding people that you are available to serve them.

> **Key Point:** Make sure your ambassadors represent you well.

Your client newsletter should project the right appearance. It's better to spend a few extra dollars to get it typeset and printed on good quality paper with rather brief and elementary articles than to spend extra hours writing long, technically correct, scholarly pieces that no one but another professional would understand.

The same principles apply to your brochures, proposals, announcements, and any other tangible products you provide to your clients or referral sources. What images do they leave with the reader?

Because prospective clients have little means of judging your internal quality, they rely on surrogates when choosing a new professional firm. Large organizations often interview or request proposals from several firms before selecting a new one. The problem is that they really don't know what they're doing when they pick "the best qualified firm." So they use any available means to reduce the bewildering number of alternatives and make their choice easier. That's why they ask for written proposals. Prospects use these proposals and brochures, not to choose a professional, but to eliminate some firms from further consideration.

> **Key Point:** A good brochure or proposal won't get you any clients, but a bad one can put you out of the running.

Souvenirs

Managing the tangibles also means to manage the tangible evidence or representation of the service—the "souvenir" as I call it. Because clients cannot hold your services in their hands like a manufactured product, they tend to pay special attention to the souvenirs as clues to your service quality. Depending on your profession, your souvenirs might include reports, documents, drawings, contracts, or financial statements. To clients, the quality of the souvenir indicates the quality of the service.

Depending on your profession, your clients may pay thousands of dollars for your services, and often all they have to show for it is a few pieces of paper containing your report. Accountants, management consultants, pension consultants, financial consultants, and lawyers frequently charge large fees for rendering opinions of various types. The value is in the opinion, not the physical report. But the physical report is the souvenir; it represents your clients' hard-earned dollars. Make sure your report shows off its value. Use heavy paper covers if you have the document bound. Consider having your firm's logo *blind embossed* (raised stamping in the paper without ink) on the cover page, or have your firm's name engraved in the center at the bottom. Your graphics designer can show you samples.

Many professionals use so-called raised printing, which is called "thermography." *Thermography* is a process of printing with a special ink that bubbles up when exposed to heat. The newly printed sheets are passed under a flame and the ink bubbles to create the raised print. It is almost always shiny and of uneven texture. Printers will tell you "it's just like engraving, only cheaper." It's not. It is cheap, and it looks cheap. The difference in cost between true engraving and thermography is minuscule when considered over a year or more. After buying the dies, the printing cost is only a few pennies more per sheet.

Never order printing from a mail-order catalog. Get a good graphics house to design your logo, letterhead, and other printing so that all printed items bearing your name present a uniform image to the public. This includes envelopes, mailing labels, business cards, door signs, and note paper. You'll be glad you did.

Questions To Think About:

- What do your business cards and stationery say about you? Are they distinctive? Or do they look like everybody else's?

- How do you visually present reports and documents?

- Your clients pay hundreds or thousands of dollars for your services. Mostly, those services are intangible. The only physical evidence of the service is the written report. Does your report show its value?

- Where do you get your client newsletter produced? What sort of appearance does it project?

- Who writes your proposals, and how much care do the writers devote to them?

Office Facilities and Equipment

What sort of image does your office project? Consider the series of images of your office that a client or prospect gets. Close your eyes if you wish.

Start with the view from the street. Your office building should present an image consistent with the way you want to be perceived. Your parking lot can be convenient and inviting, or it can be awkward, inconvenient, even threatening. It should be well lit to contribute to a feeling of security. It should be cleaned often. What is the first thing a prospective client sees when entering your office building? There might be something you can do to improve your building lobby, even if you are only a tenant. Why not ask the landlord? The worst the landlord can do is say "no." Don't forget the view that prospects see when they enter from the rear of the building.

Your listing on the building directory should compare favorably with the other companies in your building. List all the professionals in your firm on the building directory, as well as any department heads, such as firm administrator, data processing chief, etc. The longer your listing, the better.

Pay attention to what clients see when they walk down the hallway to your office entrance. These images should compare favorably with your competitors.

Prospects entering your reception area should be pleasantly surprised and favorably impressed. Your reception furniture gives prospects their most powerful initial impressions. Is your reception area conservative, progressive, expensive, cheap, first class, or "I decorated it myself"?

The works of art on your walls should be consistent with one another and with your firm's image, as well as in good taste. If possible, have the artwork be related to your profession in some tasteful way, or you could feature original art of local artists or local scenes.

> **Practical Tip:** You can obtain original art at reasonable prices from local art festivals where many artists work in their own booths, and they are usually negotiable on prices—particularly if you are interested in several works of art.

Picture your own office equipment and furniture in your mind as if you were a client. Imagine your office as if you were seeing it for the first time. Do you like what you see? Does it present an appropriate image to your clients? What changes, if any, should you make?

Your car should present an image of success. Naturally, it should be clean and polished.

The magazines in your reception area can demonstrate a concern for your clients' interests. Your professional journals are okay, but they shouldn't be the only thing for clients to read. If you are in a financial profession, be sure to include *Fortune*, *Forbes*, or *Inc.* If you cater to small business, *Inc.* is essential.

NOTES

1. Bert Decker, *Speak to Win* (audiocassette), Nightingale-Conant Corporation, Chicago, 1985.
2. Buck Rogers, *The IBM Way*, New York: Harper & Row, 1986, p. 81.

III

How to Get Better Grades on Your "Invisible Report Card"

Many practices experience a "natural" turnover of 10–20 percent of their clients each year. Some turnover is inevitable, as people die or move or businesses close their doors. But some of it isn't. If you can improve your invisible report cards, client loyalty will increase, and your client turnover will decline. Furthermore, your referrals from existing clients will increase.

Part III gives you many ideas and tools to achieve both goals. Most of the ideas will seem obvious once I point them out to you. But it was also "obvious" for thousands of years that heavy objects fell faster than light ones. Aristotle thought so, and for centuries no one ever put his conclusion to the test. Finally, in the Renaissance, Galileo Galilei is said to have taken a cannon ball and a musket ball to the top of the leaning Tower of Pisa and dropped them over the side. What was "obvious" turned out to be false.

I tell this story to make the point that everything in this part has also been researched and tested. These data are not only "obvious," but they are also "true."

10

Beware the Six Causes of Service Problems

Why do professionals sometimes fail to render good service? What causes professionals to miss the mark occasionally and get failing grades on their invisible report cards? Professors A. Parasuraman, Valarie A. Zeithaml, and Leonard L. Berry,[1] from Texas A & M University identified six causes of service quality problems:

1. Overlap of production and consumption; inevitable interactions between producers and consumers

2. Inadequate service to "intermediate customers"

3. Communication shortfalls

4. View of clients as statistics—seeing them as a number instead of a person

5. Short-run view of the business

6. Service proliferation and complexity

How many of your service quality problems can be traced to one or more of these six causes?

1. OVERLAPPING PRODUCTION AND CONSUMPTION OF SERVICE

"Goods are produced; services are performed," wrote John M. Rathwell.[2] Your clients may consume your services as they are being produced. For example, while you are meeting with and advising your client, your client is consuming your service. Your client is in your service "factory." Mistakes made in such an atmosphere are immediately apparent to your clients, and no amount of post hoc "quality control" can remanufacture, recall, or rescind them.

While your clients are waiting in the reception area, they are "consuming" the services of your receptionist. When your receptionist offers your clients a cup of coffee—or fails to offer a cup—your clients remember it as a "coffee stain" or a "Kleenex® box" experience. If your receptionist has a bad day, your clients will know it; it's not hidden in a factory somewhere.

Machine-produced products are highly uniform. Labor-intensive services can vary each time they are performed. Consider the varying quality of service between waiters at a restaurant you regularly patronize. So even if you or your associates do a good job for one client on Monday, you might perform a similar service differently on Tuesday for the same or a different client.

In some professions, the service personnel with whom clients interact (receptionists, technicians, nurses, and clerks, for example) are among the firm's least educated, lowest paid, and least respected people. If a worker in a manufacturing plant has language difficulties, is poorly dressed, has an abrasive personality, or has body odor, the customer will never know it. But with professional services, every worker's language, dress, personality, and body odors are part of the professional experience.

Practical Tips:

- Try to have the same personnel handle the same clients each time. Their familiarity with a particular client's expectations will impart more consistency to their performance.

- Reduce the number of different people with whom a particular client interacts while being serviced. The more people a client comes into contact with, the greater the chance of an unsatisfactory experience.

- If possible, perform error-prone portions of your service outside the client's presence (planning, review, typing, etc.). In this way, mistakes made during those processes have a greater chance of being caught and fixed without the client becoming aware of them. On the other hand, professionals have difficulty with clients understanding all that is done for them, so having the professional be visibly working for the client's benefit can have a positive effect on building a perception of value.

2. INADEQUATE SERVICE TO "INTERMEDIATE CUSTOMERS"

This refers to the quality of operational support provided to your frontline personnel. For example, travel agents or airline reservationists cannot serve you when their computers are down. They are "intermediate customers" of the computer maintenance people. A professional firm has intermediate customers, too. If any of your operational support falls down, your frontline people have a difficult time rendering high-quality service. But to your clients, the frontline people *are* the firm. When something goes wrong, such as a missing letter, a telephone call not returned, a document delivered late, a deadline missed, it is the frontline person—who may be totally blameless—whom the client holds responsible.

Practical Tips:

- Train your telephone operator to take accurate messages and relay them promptly to the right person in your office.

- Make sure your updates to any loose-leaf information services in your library are filed immediately so that your personnel have the most recent information available.

- Keep client files up to date, and file them promptly so that you can find work papers and correspondence when you need them.

- Consistently use the same delivery service for sending documents (such as reports) to your clients so that you become a major customer of their delivery service.

3. COMMUNICATION SHORTFALLS

Three distinct types of problems occur: (1) the firm overpromises; (2) the firm fails to stay in touch; or (3) the client's communication is misunderstood. The client may feel, "They can't be trusted or relied on," "I got no response," or "My professional doesn't listen to me. My instructions were not followed."

Overpromising to Clients

Has this ever happened to you? An assistant tells a client that he or she will have a document delivered "first thing in the morning." The client calls you at 11:30 the next morning to ask when your day starts. This is *overpromising*.

Overpromising is a major cause of client dissatisfaction. It's easy for us to promise to have a particular item handled by tomorrow. It makes the client happy (when we say it). It costs us nothing to make the promise (at the time). It is what the client likes to hear.

> Business promises are made all the time, and almost as often they're broken—needlessly creating a horrible impression. If you *say* you're going to do something, *do it*. If you can't do it, think it's more trouble than it's worth, or don't want to do it, then *don't say you will*. Make up any excuse, but don't even say "I'll try." At the very least that leaves the other party with the impression that you tried—and *failed*. [emphasis in the original]
>
> *Mark H. McCormack*[3]

Failing to Stay in Touch with Clients

A disproportionate number of service quality problems seem to arise from professionals' failure to stay in touch with clients until a problem is resolved.

Examples:

- A client of an accounting firm gets an IRS notice that a Form 1099 doesn't agree with the client's tax return. The notice includes a bill for $700 of additional income tax due. The accountant knows that there is no tax due and that the notice can be answered by providing a missing identification number on the client's return. The accountant therefore feels no need to respond quickly and fails to notify the client until two days later.

- A lawyer's client receives a jury duty notice that commands her to be in court on a certain date. The date falls in the middle of a planned two-week cruise to celebrate her 25th wedding anniversary. The client—who has never been called for jury duty before—calls in tears about ruining her anniversary. The lawyer knows it is a simple matter to arrange for the jury duty to be scheduled after the cruise, but the lawyer fails to call the client until a more challenging case has been handled.

- A patient calls his doctor's nurse complaining about a rash on his left arm. He has read somewhere that this is a possible sign of leprosy. The doctor knows it is probably a side effect of the prescription he is taking, but the doctor doesn't return the patient's call until after seeing all the patients scheduled for that day.

This sort of thing happens all the time—to the accountant or lawyer or doctor. They are routine—to the accountant or lawyer or doctor. But these are events of *earthshaking importance to the client or patient!* Receipt of *any* notice from the IRS or the court strikes fear and terror in the hearts of some clients. They may act pretty calm about it, but their guts are turning over until they get the "all clear" from the expert. To them, these are crises comparable only to the transmission falling out of their car in the middle of a freeway at 60 miles per hour! To the professional, it's just a routine annoyance.

These situations are ripe for a "coffee stain" experience.

Misunderstanding Client Communications

Some of your personnel may talk to clients as if the clients were professionals. Your clients do not understand your professional jargon. Sometimes inexperienced staff members use professional jargon in a mistaken attempt to impress clients. It doesn't work; it only irritates them.

Practical Tips:

- Tell clients—in simple terms—what they can expect to happen in the situation.

- Tell clients what you are going to do and when, as well as when you will report back to them. Then do it.

- When something happens to interrupt your schedule, call the client *before* the due date and tell them you have been delayed and when they can expect to hear from you again.

Occasionally, your clients may not understand how to get service. They may have to run through an organizational maze to get serviced. "That's not in this department; you'll have to call accounting," is an all too common answer. If you are forcing clients to learn your organization to have their problems solved, you may need to evaluate and modify the training of your frontline people so that they can handle requests directly. Otherwise, analyze and revise your client orientation procedures so that your clients are *gently* trained how to interact with the various departments in the firm.

4. VIEW OF CLIENTS AS STATISTICS

The client deals with only a few professionals—perhaps a lawyer, an accountant, an insurance agent, a stock broker, and a banker. This means that your typical client can remember every important contact they have had with you in the past year.

But you deal with hundreds or even thousands of clients. Can you remember every important contact you have with all your clients? Of course not, because they outnumber you.

Services are performed for individuals—even services to corporate clients. It can be very difficult to keep this perspective in mind when you see 40 patients a day, or handle 85 collection actions a month, or process 950 individual income tax returns, or do monthly bookkeeping for 65 small businesses, or have 125 clients a month visit your office.

When you have many clients, you can too easily begin to view them as statistics. You can overlook opportunities to present individualized service. Sometimes you see so many of the same type of problem that you lose your sensitivity to the client's perceptions. For example, $100 doesn't seem as important as $1,000, but it is critical to the client who is out the $100.

Remember the 1099 mismatch? The jury notice? The rash? When a client telephones you with such a problem and it is the 25th such telephone call you have received this month, the potential for treating clients as a statistic—and for them to be disappointed—is quite high.

Practical Tips:

- Train your receptionist (and yourself) to call all clients by name.

- Avoid using client account numbers externally, even if you use them for internal accounting.

- After each client contact, write a note to the file on personal matters discussed, such as children's names, trips taken, and other personal information important to your client.

- Ask your secretary to automatically fetch the current file and billing file for any client who telephones you and to place it on your desk. Refresh your memory by referring to it before picking up the telephone or as you speak to the client.

- Mention personal items about each client you talk to.

---

5. SHORT-RUN VIEW OF THE BUSINESS

Too much emphasis on short-term profitability will adversely affect quality. For example, reducing the number of telephone lines increases the number of times your clients get a busy signal. Reducing the number of typists increases the time it takes to get documents typed. A bank could reduce the number of tellers and increase the length of its lines.

A customer of one company said, "They have the best product support in the world before you buy. Once you buy and sign the check, the service goes down the drain."

The short-run view of conducting a business can be a particularly serious problem in professional firms. Historically, most professions had low capital requirements, and professional services were delivered primarily by individual effort. But today's professionals have word processors, microcomputers, electronic telephones, fax machines, and on and on and on. The capital requirements today in many professions would have been inconceivable a generation ago. But old habits die hard, and many professionals still try to operate their practices on a shoestring. They will do without an extra computer terminal. They will buy a cheaper—and slower—printer. They will delay adding an extra employee or an extra telephone line as long as possible. But if you jeopardize the *service* in a service business, you jeopardize the *business*.

It's almost as if some firms are so busy chopping down trees that they won't invest the time to sharpen their ax (training of personnel in new techniques), or the money to buy a chain saw (investment in training and equipment costs). As a result, they continue to do things the old way and do not take advantage of new developments and new technology and perhaps respond too slowly to changes in their business environment.

6. SERVICE PROLIFERATION AND COMPLEXITY

Professional firms nowadays must cope with too many new services in too short a period of time and with too much added complexity in existing services. The following are only a few of the myriad changes:

- Personal financial planning
- Tax Reform Act of 1986
- New consulting areas
- Leveraged buy-outs
- New surgical procedures
- Changes in laws
- New medicines
- New regulations

Often, change outstrips the firm's capacity to handle it.

Some firms "jump on the band wagon" and start marketing a new service to their clients even before they are fully trained and prepared to deliver it. This is just one more opportunity for things to go wrong.

A big problem in some firms is "partner jealousy." Some partners insist on doing everything for "their" clients. They jealously guard the client relationship and refuse to allow anyone else to service "their" clients. As a result, such partners would need to be expert in every facet of their profession, no matter how esoteric or sophisticated. With the complexities and necessary specializations in every profession today, this causes a shortfall in service to clients because the firm is not able to offer them the broad range of expertise they really need. Such partners fail to take advantage of the benefits of belonging to a firm: Each partner does not have to be expert in all areas.

NOTES

1. A. Parasuraman, Valarie A. Zeithaml, and Leonard L. Berry, "Quality Counts in Services, Too," *Business Horizons*, May/June 1985, pp. 47–49.
2. John M. Rathwell, *Marketing in the Service Sector*, Cambridge, MA: Winthrop Publishers, 1974, p. 58.
3. Mark H. McCormack, *What They Don't Teach You at Harvard Business School*, New York: Bantam Books, 1984, pp. 36–37.

11

How to Manage Your "Moments of Truth"

PROFESSIONAL RELATIONSHIPS

The marriage between a client and [a professional] is not, alas, an equal, modern, enlightened one. Rather, it should be compared to a Victorian marriage in which one party (the client) expects to be catered to in exchange for providing the means of support of the other party (in this case, the professional service firm).

The client, like the stereotypical Victorian husband, has sought out a partner who is expected to be loyal, faithful, supportive and caring. And, above all, accommodating. The responsibility for the success of the relationship . . . falls almost entirely to the wife. In the client–[professional] marriage, no matter who is at fault, restoring peace and harmony in the wake of a conflict is the [professional's] problem.

David Maister[1]

Though the relationships between professionals and their clients only begin when the sale is made, such relationships intensify once the buying decision has been made. In fact, once the actual service commences, professional services can continue for weeks, months, or even years. The quality of the relationship determines whether clients will seek the professional again the next time they need professional services.

As Theodore Levitt[2] says, "The sale merely consummates the courtship. Then the marriage begins. How good the marriage is depends on how well the relationship is managed by the seller." Sometimes divorce is impossible, as when a major lawsuit, registration statement, construction project, etc. is in progress. However, if the professional treats the client as "another case to a busy practitioner," the relationship will be damaged, and the client may not return. You should manage client relationships from the very beginning. Levitt concludes, "To get out the marriage manual after trouble has begun is to have done so too late."

Traditional marketing gets the client in the door the first time; relationship management keeps the client coming back again and again. Traditional marketing is the courtship; relationship management is the marriage.

Because production and consumption are partly simultaneous, you need to develop two distinctly different types of marketing to clients. The first is *traditional marketing* to bring in new clients. The second is *interactive marketing*, which is what your frontline personnel and other resources such as your tangibles are doing every time a client interacts with them. See Figure 12.[3]

Interactive marketing requires special attention to the unique feature that distinguishes a relationship from a transaction: *time*.

Winning and keeping clients depend on rewarding people for being clients. Your frontline personnel are immediately responsible for giving

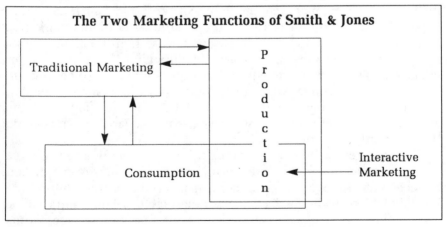

Figure 12

your clients a rewarding experience during your service parade. Therefore, they have an immense impact on whether the client comes back. Your frontline personnel and your souvenirs may be the little extras that make your service outstanding in comparison with your competitors.

Every moment of truth will make clients feel a little better, a little worse, or about the same about your firm. If the experience was rewarding, the chances are that they will come back for more and perhaps recommend you to others. If the event was an ordeal, they probably won't be back, and they may tell up to 20 other people what a lousy experience they had to endure.

Whether your frontline personnel realize it or not, they are marketing your firm whenever they interact with clients. Once your marriage to a new client begins, the quality of the relationship depends on how well *you* manage it. The natural tendency of relationships, whether in business or in marriage, is to deteriorate. Almost always, sensitivity and attentiveness erode.

Because of this tendency to deteriorate, client relationships must be continually recreated anew at each moment of truth. Even though many nonpartners are on the front line, the chief responsibility for maintaining and enhancing those relationships is the partners'.

It is no surprise that partners are usually rated and rewarded according to the client relationships they control. Those relationships, like any asset, can appreciate or depreciate, depending on how well they are managed.

Maintaining and strengthening client relationships are not just a matter of good manners, charm, "blue smoke," and "mirrors." Truly expert "client handlers" possess more than just traditional marketing skills because their function transcends what traditional marketing usually does. Remember that external quality alone is insufficient for client satisfaction; the requisite internal quality must also be present. To enhance and reinforce the client bonds require good management of both the internal operations devoted to the clients' affairs and the external quality of the clients' service experience. Partners who can do this are richly rewarded.

For best results, such relationship management should have firmwide programs for maintenance, investment, improvement, and replacement. But even in mediocre firms, certain partners intuitively know how to bring home the bacon for their clients. The results can be spectacular. Good quality service—and all that those three words imply—is the key.

THE TEN COMMANDMENTS OF GOOD BUSINESS

Reznick, Fedder & Silverman (RF&S) celebrated its tenth anniversary with more than 200 people on its payroll. When I asked Dave Reznick what makes his firm different, he replied: "We don't have the patent on Vaseline. If our clients want to buy services of the type we render, there are any number of firms offering similar services. What makes us different is two things: We are accurate, and we care about our clients. When clients come to us, they know our product will be correct technically, and they also know we really care for their well-being." Dave's attitude permeates RF&S. They are absolute *fanatics* about high-quality service.

At every staff meeting, Reznick hands out copies of "The Ten Commandments of Good Business," and he has every person in the firm read them aloud. They offer some pretty good advice for professionals to follow. And the best ones do. Here they are, with "clients" substituted for "customers" in the original version:

1. Clients are the most important people in any business—in person, by mail, or by telephone.

2. Clients are not dependent on us; we are dependent on them.

3. Clients are not an interruption of our work; they are the purpose of it.

4. Clients do us a favor when they call; we are not doing them a favor by serving them.

5. Clients are a part of our business, not outsiders.

6. Clients are not cold statistics; they are flesh-and-blood human beings with feelings and emotions like our own.

7. Clients are not people to argue or match wits with. Nobody ever won an argument with a client.

8. Clients are people who bring us their wants; it is our job to fill those wants profitably to them and to us.

9. Clients are the life blood of this and every business.

10. Clients are deserving of the most courteous and attentive treatment we can give them.

Shotz, Miller & Glusman in Philadelphia grew to 100 people in their first six years of existence. Steve Shotz told me, "We may lose a client over fees, but we never want to lose one because of bad service. I don't mind a former client telling people we are expensive, but I don't want anyone walking the streets of Philadelphia saying we wouldn't return their phone calls."

Managing those moments of truth to enhance the client relationship is more important to preserving and enhancing your intangible asset—goodwill—than is the management of your tangible assets. Managing moments of truth is hard, which is why you must work on it diligently. You should regularly and seriously ask yourself, How am I doing with this client? Is the relationship improving or declining? Am I keeping my promises? What am I neglecting? How does our firm compare with our competitors?

Consultant Chris Frederiksen recommends that associates complete a "happiness questionnaire" after each interaction with a client. The happiness questionnaire is a report from the associate to the partner in charge of the client relationship, in which the associate answers four simple questions:

1. Is the client happy?

2. Is partner TLC (tender loving care) needed?

3. Have we asked the client for more work?

4. Have we asked the client for referrals?

Table 2[4] lists some partner behaviors that affect client relationships.

As Levitt[5] points out, "One of the surest signs of a bad or declining relationship is the absence of complaints. . . . Nobody is ever *that* satisfied, especially not over an extended period of time. [Clients are] either not being candid or not being contacted."

The problem and the challenge are that many moments of truth take place far beyond the immediate control of the partners. Because partners cannot be there to influence the quality of so many moments of truth, they have to learn to manage them indirectly through their associates by creating a client-centered culture and work environment that reinforces the value of putting the client first.

Improving the *internal* quality of your work can be expensive and almost impossible to demonstrate to your clients, so you don't get credit for superior internal quality. But improving the *external* quality of your work is usually very inexpensive and infinitely more visible to clients.

Table 2
Partner Behaviors That Affect Client Relationships

Good	Bad
Initiate positive phone calls	Make only callbacks
Make recommendations	Make justifications
Speak candidly	Accommodative language
Use the telephone	Use letters when phone calls would be better
Show appreciation	Wait for misunderstandings
Make service suggestions	Wait for service requests
Use "we" problem-solving language	Use "owe-us" legal language
Anticipate problems	Respond only to problems
Use easily understood language	Use jargon
Confront personality problems	Hide personality problems
Talk of "our future together"	Talk of making good on the past
Routinize responses	Fire drill/emergency responses
Accept responsibility	Shift blame
Plan the future	Rehash the past

Six basic steps help you to earn higher grades from your clients:

1. Discover what your clients need and want.

2. Manage client expectations.

3. Manage the tangibles.

4. Manage the firm's personnel.

5. Be the best at handling problems.

6. Regularly communicate with your clients what you are doing for them.

Key Point: Remember that you need to work on the intermediate service providers as well as your frontline people. You can't send a carpenter to build a house without providing a saw, a hammer, and nails. Your intermediate service providers—your support personnel—are vital in providing the proper tools and materials to your front line.

NOTES

1. David Maister, "Lessons in Client-Loving," *Architectural Technology*, Fall 1985, p. 48.
2. Theodore Levitt, *The Marketing Imagination*, New York: Free Press, 1986, pp. 111, 115.
3. Adapted from Grönroos, 1983, p. 62. Used with permission of the publisher.
4. Adapted from Levitt, 1986, p. 119. Used with permission of the publisher.
5. Levitt, p. 119.

12

How to Manage Client Expectations and Perceptions

Because your clients buy solutions to problems (not professional services per se), you must discover just exactly what problem the client wants you to solve. In addition, because clients also buy good feelings, you must be concerned with the manner in which your service is delivered.

FIND OUT WHAT THE CLIENT NEEDS AND WANTS

Clients are like a bird in the hand: grasp them too tightly and you will crush them; grasp them too loosely and they will fly away.

David W. Cottle

Therefore, you must consider two aspects of each client's needs: service outcome and operating style. Too often, professionals concentrate on providing what they think are their clients' desired service outcomes and neglect their clients' operating style considerations.

Service outcomes are the solutions the clients want—what they are trying to accomplish. Service outcomes are the standards by which your efforts will be judged, so you need to find out how clients will decide whether you have achieved their desired results.

Operating style refers to the manner of delivery: How do your clients want you to proceed? Operating style includes many client-interaction factors: How closely do they want you to confer with them? How much do they want to know? How much freedom of operation do they want to allow you?

Different clients need different degrees of communication, empathy, and assurance. You need to know which clients need how much guidance. Some very self-reliant clients want you to give them all the facts, lay out all the options, and let them decide. Some clients want all of those, and, in addition, they want your recommendation, which they may or may not take. Other clients want you to tell them just enough so that they know you know what you're talking about. Then they want your recommendation, which they will almost always take.

Sometimes, you can give clients too many options. Michael LeBoeuf[1] tells of the time he went to an eye doctor because of blurred vision in one eye. After an examination, the doctor determined the cause. Instead of recommending a course of action, he recited all the available options. Even when LeBoeuf asked him to do so, the doctor wouldn't recommend one.

> I left his office feeling frustrated. I went to him with a problem and I wanted a solution. I didn't want a discourse on the state of the art of contact lenses. I wanted to see better. Although I couldn't express it at the time, a little voice inside me was saying, "Dammit, you're the doctor. . . . Make a decision. If you lead, I'll follow." Yet the man in charge wouldn't take charge. A friend of mine had a similar experience with the same doctor, and both of us have since taken our eye care needs elsewhere.

Key Point: The first rule for happy clients: Give them what they want.

How do you find out what they want? Ask the right questions. You can't help your clients if you don't know what service outcomes they want. To oversimplify: You want to ask each client, "What is your situation now?" and "What would you like it to be?" This is the pure essence of finding out the client's problem. In practice, it's not quite as easy because clients often don't how to describe their current situation in meaningful terms. Also, they frequently don't know what is doable in the professional realm.

Use open-ended, nonthreatening questions, and encourage the client to talk. When you hear something you need to know more about, ask, "Can you tell me more about that?" If you need to know how much the client wants to spend, be sure you explain that you need the information in order to tailor your services to the client's needs. Here are examples of open-ended questions:

- What do you hope my services will help you to accomplish? Or how would you like this service engagement to end?

- What do you know about the way we work?

- How much authority do I have to make commitments for you without consulting you?

- How often do you want me to confer with you?

- How soon do you need this?

- How can we be of greatest help to you?

Because all professional engagements are cooperative efforts between your firm and your client, the client has to do some of the work. Sometimes, the client's only work is to give you basic information at the initial conference; from there on, you're on your own. Sometimes, however, the client must participate actively at every step of the process, such as in building a client's personal residence. Sometimes, you can use the client's labor to lower your fees, as in gathering data from third parties, organizing information, or doing legwork. Find out how much cooperation you can expect from the client.

Naturally, tradeoffs are involved for both you and the client. Some clients with large staffs may want to do as much of the work as possible.

Examples:

- A corporate attorney's client may want her or his own in-house legal staff to handle all of the routine aspects of the case.

- A large developer's architect may want the developer's own drafting department to prepare renderings, make models, or do other parts of the work, to reduce the independent architects' fees.

- One CPA's business client may have a controller to close the year-end books while another may prefer to have the CPA do it.

Key Point: In planning each service commitment or project with a client, obtain a clear mutual understanding with the client as to your responsibilities and the client's responsibilities.

Your goal is to have a complete mental grasp of the client's circumstances, thoughts, feelings, hopes, and fears about this situation so that you can act in the client's best interests and stay within the client's financial means.

One of the key items both in understanding the specific client and in communicating in general is the ability to listen to the client. *Good listening* is *more than* just *staying awake.* Poor listening has many causes, including

- Distractions caused by the speaker's appearance or mannerisms, particularly if unpleasant to you

- Distractions caused by external factors, such as noise, light, and movement

- A person who speaks excessively, loudly, softly, indistinctly, or ambiguously

- Inattention to the speaker, letting other subjects cross your mind

- Emotional distraction due to becoming angry or upset because you disagree with the speaker's views

- Loss of interest because you have heard it all before

- Mental distraction caused by thinking of your next question or comment

---

Practical Tips to improve listening:

- Look at people when they talk to you and when you talk to them.

- Sit up straight and be alert.

- Let people complete their thoughts without interruption.

- Give nonverbal feedback by nodding or smiling when appropriate.

- Confirm your understanding of what the speaker has said by repeating your paraphrase of the speaker's words.

MANAGE CLIENT EXPECTATIONS

Clients actually buy expectations of benefits that you promised them, or that they *think* you promised them. When it takes a long time to fulfill the promise, or if fulfillment is a continuous process taking a long time, clients' anxieties can build. Several things can increase clients' anxiety:

- When clients suspect that you do not completely understand their requirements, they think you are wasting their time and money.

- The more complex the service being performed, the less they understand what you are doing and why. Mysteries always seem threatening to people; they feel better when they know what is going on.

- The more operating procedures, management routines, and service activities they must participate in, the more likely they will feel frustrated.

- If the performance of the service takes longer than they expected, they will become uncertain about the final outcome.

- The more personnel they must interact with, the lower their satisfaction.

A key factor to increase your chances for an interactive marketing "win" is to help the client form realistic expectations of (a) the nature of the service you will perform, (b) the moments of truth they will experience, and (c) the outcome you will achieve.

A few things can help you to exert a little more control over new clients' expectations—and old clients' for that matter:

1. Avoid the promotional temptation to overpromise.

2. Learn to spot extremist clients in advance.

3. Don't oversell the service outcome.

4. Scale down the client's expectations.

5. Introduce the client to the idea of multiple factors.

6. Educate the client and the client's family and other advisors.

7. Stay in touch with the client throughout the service process.

1. Avoid Overpromising

Promising "fast, friendly service at all times" creates considerably different client expectations than saying "We do our best to serve you, even when we're busy."

Don't let your client think you are a superhero; you just create higher hurdles you have to jump to impress them. If they think you are perfect, they will be disappointed when you make a mistake. And mistakes *will* happen.

Making unrealistic promises may get you more business initially, but it raises unrealistic expectations, and it unbalances the service quality equation. This invariably leads to client disappointment and discourages word-of-mouth referrals.

> The world is divided into two classes of people: the few people who make good on their promises (even if they don't promise as much) and the many who don't. Get in column A and stay there. You'll be very valuable wherever you are.
>
> *Robert Townsend*[2]

Do you remember Holiday Inn's "no surprises" advertising campaign of 1986? It promised, "The best surprise is no surprise." It was dropped because it raised unrealistic expectations that the company could not deliver on.

Key Point: For a professional, it is far better to exceed client expectations than to let clients down.

One successful partner revealed to me the simple secret of his success. He said, "I always get clients' reports to them one day before they are expecting it." In other words, if he could get the report to the client by the 17th of the month, he promised it for the 19th. Then, even if he ran into trouble, he delivered it on the 18th and exceeded the client's expectations.

2. Spot Extremists

There are two kinds of extremist clients: those who think you can do no wrong; and those who think you do everything wrong. Either way, you're sure to lose if you deal with them.

Extremist clients place the entire responsibility for performance of your service on your shoulders. However, though you certainly bear the chief burden of responsibility for your service, if you get good cooperation from your clients, it is easier to give good service. In fact, every service is a cooperative effort that is influenced to some extent by the client's input: garbage in; garbage out. Extremist clients don't realize this. In fact, the hallmark of extremist clients is abdication of their part in the responsibility for a successful outcome to your professional efforts.

The first kind of extremist client has an almost messianic faith in you. I call them "Pollyannas" because of their unrealistic attitude of "I'm not the least bit worried; I know you won't let me down" even when the prognosis is not good. The Pollyanna flatters your ego. You think: They really have confidence in me. But you are being set up for a fall, because a Pollyanna's expectations are so unrealistically high that not even a superhero could meet them.

How do you recognize them? Here are a few warning signs of potential Pollyannas:

- They think you are a genius.

- They are unsophisticated about your profession.

- They think computers or other technology or quick fix will solve all their problems in the office.

- They think the pill you prescribed will cure them instantly.

- They think you know every word of the applicable law by heart and have memorized all the relevant cases.

- They think your personal financial planning will prevent any of their investments from losing money.

In short: They think your skills will guarantee a successful solution to their problem.

The other kind of extremist client cannot be satisfied no matter what you do. I call them "Oscars" after Oscar the Grouch on the TV show, *Sesame Street*. They complain about everything, and they are never satisfied. Here are a few identifying marks to help you recognize Oscars:

- They had unrealistic expectations of their former professional.

- They change professionals frequently.

- They bad-mouth their former professional unnecessarily.

- They may be screwballs or flakes.

- They are unreasonably demanding.

- They chronically complain about life in general.

- They tend to procrastinate or bring fragmented information or incomplete data and expect you to achieve a good result.

Of the two, I prefer Pollyannas to Oscars; you may be able to educate Pollyannas and bring them down to earth. There is not much you can do with Oscars except refer them to your worst enemy. Forewarned is forearmed.

3. Don't Oversell

If you promise the moon, it is reasonable for customers to expect it.

Theodore Levitt[3]

Be careful what you say when explaining to clients what you hope to accomplish for them.

Examples:

- "Though my tax advice is sound and well-documented, the IRS could disagree with the position I have recommended."

- "Computers will not solve problems created by inaccurate recordkeeping."

- "Though our staff is top-notch, no one is invulnerable to making mistakes."

Don't promise the client more than you—and your staff—can deliver. Even though you don't give any guarantee a particular result will be achieved, the implication is that "dotting the i's and crossing the t's" will assure a favorable outcome.

4. Scale Down Client Expectations

Watch what you say. Don't say "you're home free" when you mean "it looks pretty good." For example, your completion of the loan presentation package does *not* assure the loan will be approved. Your presence during negotiations does not mean a deal will be struck. Computerization may give the client more and better information, but it probably will not reduce cost. And so on.

The key is to anticipate the client's expectations and deal with them in advance. Discuss any possible roadblocks or delays at the earliest possible moment. Make it clear how you will respond and what the client can expect.

Irwin Steinberg, a Chicago partner with Friedman, Eisenstein, Raemer & Schwartz put it best: "Play the offense, not the defense." As soon as you know or can anticipate you will have a problem, take the initiative to call the client in advance. Don't wait for the client to call you.

5. Introduce the Idea of Multiple Factors

The outcome of your efforts on behalf of clients is affected by many things outside your control, such as:

- Actions of the IRS, Congress, and the Courts in regard to taxes

- Decisions of appellate courts in regard to legal precedents

- Zoning board actions in proposed real estate developments or construction projects

- The patient's lifestyle in medical matters

- Conditions of site and subsoil in architectural matters

- The client's own management style and skills in regard to consultation recommendations

Similarly, bankers, brokers, suppliers, and the actions of the client and the client's personnel will have impact on your results.

> **Key Point:** Emphasize that you can *influence* events, but you cannot *control* them.

6. Educate Client and Client's Advisors

Help your clients by educating them. Knowledgeable clients make better decisions, provide better input, and thus gain greater satisfaction. Client education takes several forms.

Some clients can be educated to perform certain services themselves.

Examples:

- A corporate lawyer could train clients as to the types of matters to document in the corporate minutes.

- A doctor could train patients in good eating and exercise habits.

- A dentist could train patients how to reduce plaque buildup.

- A CPA firm could educate its clients to prepare income tax organizers to make the income tax preparation task easier.

You can also educate clients as to when they need your services. This helps clients know when they need professional assistance and when they do not.

Examples:

- A law firm could send clients a brochure on "When to Update Your Will."

- A CPA firm could feature a newsletter article on when to update the client's estate plan.

- Veterinarians might include articles on pet care and "when to see the Vet" in their newsletters.

You can also educate clients as to how to use your services most effectively.

Examples:

- Chiropractors might have pamphlets on care of the neck and spine.

- The income tax organizer might also be a checklist of information for clients to gather to assist the accountant.

- Doctors often have printed flyers that explain to patients how to take a particular prescription.

The last form of especially helpful education is to explain to clients the underlying reason for policies or procedures that could frustrate them. Again, "Play the offense; not the defense."

Examples:

- Once the client conference is held regarding drafting a client's will, the attorney might explain why it may take two weeks to prepare the final document.

- The CPA who prepares a request for an income tax refund might explain to the client how long it will take for the refund to arrive.

- The dentist might explain to a patient why it takes so long to make a crown.

- The architect might educate clients as to how long a change order takes and all of the steps necessary to implement the design changes that clients have authorized.

---

7. Stay in Touch

Nothing is worse to a client than "wondering about. . . ." Often, professionals accept an assignment from a client and go charging off on their white horses to slay the dragon. But it may be weeks or months until you come back with the dragon's head. In the meantime, the client is worried the dragon may appear while you are gone.

One professional I spoke with describes his techniques as follows: "Whenever I reach a decision point, I call the client, lay out the alternatives, make a recommendation, then ask for his opinion and instructions. Ninety-nine percent of the time, he tells me to do what I was going to do anyway. But it makes him feel good to be consulted, and he is taking direct responsibility for specific expenditures and time-consuming activities. He is never surprised by what I got up to on his behalf, and he is constantly informed as to what I'm doing for him. If I don't have a decision for him to make, I call him anyway just to let him know what the status is. *And every conversation ends with two sentences: I ask if there's anything else he wants me to do, and I tell him when I'll next call him."* [emphasis added][4]

Some clients may not want to hear from you so often, but find out the clients' preferences and follow them. After all, they are the ones paying the bill.

Practical Tips:

- Follow up client meetings with a brief letter or memo summarizing the discussion and any decisions made.

- Find out the client's real deadlines and meet them—or beat them.

- Send the client copies of all correspondence you have with third parties regarding the client's affairs.

Another example of playing the offense is to initiate contact as soon as you know that a client is going to be disappointed. For example, when a job will be delayed, when the cost is more than you originally estimated, or when you or someone else made a mistake that may annoy the client, don't wait for the client to call you. If you wait, you'll have an uphill battle.

When things do go wrong, apologize and take responsibility to make them go right. It's better to tell clients and take the pressure than to keep them in the dark, give them an unpleasant surprise, and perhaps lose them.

Fortunately, the way that clients react to bad news depends to a large degree on how you tell them. Don't turn clients off by telling them "no" or giving them the bad news without preamble. For example, if your fee is going to be more than you expected, don't start off by saying "This is going to cost you more than I thought." Instead, begin by explaining the facts on which you and the client were basing the original estimate, then show how those assumptions were in error (I hope that this is through no fault of yours) and the effect that this will have on your fee estimate. Remind the client that your original estimate was only an estimate, and get his or her permission before proceeding.

By following these steps in communicating with clients, educating them, and managing their expectations, you will be able to serve them in a way that will get you consistently high marks for quality, increase client loyalty, and keep them coming back for more.

MANAGE THE TANGIBLES

Managing the tangibles is closely related to managing client expectations. Managing expectations increases the chance the client will have realistic expectations *before* you render the service. In contrast, "managing the tangibles" is concerned with shaping client opinions *during and after* your rendering of the service.

The tangibles could be considered part of the "packaging" of your product. If you think this isn't important, consider this tale of packaging by Wall Street investment bankers.

> Special brass-plated, unnumbered side doors quietly admit the impressionable bigwigs with especially sought-after investment banking accounts. Heavily starched linen tablecloths, Waterford crystal, and imported chefs once apprenticed to Paul Bocuse characterize the opulent private dining rooms from which clients and prospective clients may enjoy splectacular views of the bustling city far down below. The packaging in which investment banking firms present themselves to their clients gets all the concentrated care that goes into packaging such other comparably hustled products as toiletries for the teeming masses.
>
> Both practices endure because both work. Both customers buy hopeful expectations, not actual things. The ability to satisfy those expectations is more effectively communicated by the packaging than by simple generic description of what's in the package. Feelings are more important than feeling. How we feel about a car is more important than how the car feels.[5]

Chapter 9 described how to manage your tangible "ambassadors" and "souvenirs." Recall that your ambassadors represent you all the time, and your service's souvenirs are the only things clients have to show for the fees they paid you.

Remember from Chapter 3 that most businesses come closer to meeting customer expectations on the tangibles than on any other dimension, but even the tangibles still fall short of customer expectations. Think of one of your competitors' offices that has really impressed you. Is there anything there you could adapt to your firm? Obtain samples of your competitors' ambassadors and souvenirs, or get samples from firms in other cities with whom you do not compete. How do your ambassadors and souvenirs compare with theirs? Could you learn anything from them?

NOTES

1. Michael LeBoeuf, *How to Win Customers and Keep Them for Life*, New York: G.P. Putnam's Sons, 1987, p. 105.

2. Robert Townsend, *Further Up The Organization*, New York: Harper & Row, 1970, 1984, 1988, p. 184.

3. Theodore Levitt, *The Marketing Imagination*, New York: Free Press, 1986, p. 117.

4. David Maister, "Quality Work Doesn't Mean Quality Service," *The American Lawyer*, April 1984, p. 8.

5. Levitt, 1986, p. 8.

13

The Key to Motivation

Why do you need a special program to motivate your personnel? Didn't you hire motivated people? They were well motivated when they started, reporting on day one all smiles. They were determined to make a good impression, learn their job well, perform to the top of their ability, and earn greater responsibilities. Remember what it was like when you started a new job? Come on, it wasn't *that* long ago! Your new employees today are just like you were then. Their attitude is good, they pay attention, they take their responsibilities very seriously. What happened?

> Reflect back to your childhood days when there was a school playground where a lot of fun games could be played and pleasant times had. Then introduce a couple of oversized bullies into the situation. These characters make it difficult for the rest of the people to play their games or even enjoy themselves. They work to no known rules and terrorize on a random basis. They interrupt the game, take the ball, and do whatever it is that turns them on.
>
> Suppose, in order to overcome this problem, the school executives decide to [institute] a motivation program. However, they send the victims to school, not the bullies. That is what happens in business.
>
> *Philip B. Crosby*[1]

New-hires have an emotional investment in your firm. They come to you with the "new job high." Your new employees are like you were; almost every one comes to you full of enthusiasm, idealism, dedication, and loyalty to their new firm.

And some firms beat it out of them as fast as they can.

All that most people really need to remain enthusiastic is to be involved, to know what is expected from them, to be accountable, to be acknowledged, and to be allowed to reach for their potential. But this is easier said than done.

> The issue is "How do you turn ordinary people into such turned-on persistent people?" It doesn't take genius in the executive suite. It takes respect for the individual, and ownership, and commitment.
>
> It is leadership, not management. Management is about arranging and telling. Leadership is about growing and enhancing. Too often we think of the manager as cop, referee, devil's advocate, nay-sayer, and pronouncer. Instead, the supportive, effective leader is cheerleader, enthusiast, nurturer, coach, and facilitator.
>
> *Tom Peters*

We cannot motivate other people. All we can do is create a climate in which they can thrive. Motivation is a door that can only be unlocked from inside. Also, we can never *control* other people. All we can do is control our own thoughts, emotions, actions and reactions—and thereby serve as a good example and role model.

HERE'S TO THE WINNERS!

Just as all parents consider their children to be above average, we all think we're tops. Yet many professionals take a negative view of their personnel. They berate their associates for poor performance. They call for risk taking but punish even tiny failures. As a result, such professionals don't see their personnel the way the personnel see themselves. Is it any wonder they can't communicate?

To paraphrase Peters and Waterman,[2]

> In a recent psychological survey, when a random sample of male adults were asked to rank themselves on "the ability to get along with others," *all* subjects put themselves in the top half of the

population. Sixty percent rated themselves in the top 10 percent, and 25 percent ever so humble thought they were in the top 1 percent. In leadership, 70 percent rated themselves in the top quartile; only 2 percent felt they were below average as leaders. Finally, 60 percent of males said they were in the top quartile in athletic ability; only 6 percent said they were below average.

We all think we are winners; that is our reality. We will ignore anything that conflicts with this reality. The challenge is to design personnel systems that continually reinforce this notion and help people to live up to their self-image. Excellent companies have systems that reinforce degrees of winning rather than degrees of losing. Their personnel by and large make their targets because the targets are set (often by the personnel themselves) to allow it to happen.

IBM explicitly manages to ensure that over 70 percent of its salespeople make their targets. One of their competitors works it so that only 40 percent of their personnel make target. So 70 percent of IBMers feel like winners. In the other company, 60 percent feel like losers.

> Label a man a loser and he'll start acting like one. As one GM manager noted, "Our control systems are designed under the apparent assumption that 90 percent of the people are lazy ne'er-do-wells, just waiting to lie, cheat, steal, or otherwise screw us. We demoralize 95 percent of the work force who do act as adults by designing systems to cover our tails against the 5 percent who really are bad actors."
>
> *Peters and Waterman*[3]

People typically treat any success as their own and any failure as the system's. This is consistent with most people's self-image and their view of the universe. If anything goes well, they made it happen because they see themselves as winners. If something bad happens, "It's not my fault." A bad result must have been caused by something else, outside of their control.

The implications for executives are clear. *People tune out when they feel they are failing, because they assign the cause to something other than themselves*, such as interest rates, their boss, their subordinates, the government, the union, etc. They listen only if the system leads them to believe they are (or can be) successful.

WHY POSITIVE REINFORCEMENT WORKS SO WELL

Just as people do not perceive success and failure in symmetrical terms, so too positive and negative reinforcement are not opposite sides of the same coin; they are not symmetrical. Negative reinforcement (essentially the threat of punitive sanctions) causes behavior to change in strange, unpredictable, and often undesirable ways. Furthermore, punishment does not teach anything beneficial; it only punishes. Positive reinforcement causes change, too, but usually in the desired direction. Positive reinforcement shapes behavior in predictable ways and also enhances the person's self-image and teaches the person what's wanted and appreciated. In addition, simply using positive phrasings (e.g., "Please be sure to mail that today") can better guide people than using negative ones (e.g., "Don't let that sit around until it's too late to go out in today's mail").

Examples:

- A partner disciplines an employee for "not treating a client well." How might he or she respond? Not only does the employee not know what to do to improve; he or she might respond by avoiding clients altogether. Contrary to the partner's intention, "clients" rather than "treating a client badly" has become associated with punishment.

- Another partner tells an employee: "You have acted in the best traditions of our firm in responding to Mrs. Jones's minor complaint." How might the employee respond? The reaction of the employee will likely be to beat the bushes looking for more clients to treat well.

- Picture a person handing a very full cup of coffee across your desk. On your desk are a lot of valuable papers. If you say, "Don't spill it!," what kind of mental picture will that person see? The person will have a picture of spilling a cup of coffee all over the desk and papers. But if you say, "Be careful," the person will have a mental picture of someone very skillfully handling a full cup of coffee.

Central to the whole notion of managing is the superior/subordinate relationship, the idea of manager as boss, and the corollary that orders will be issued and followed. The threat of punishment is the principal implied power that underlies it all. To the extent that this underlying notion prevails, we are not paying attention to people's dominant need to be winners.

Peters and Waterman[4]

To paraphrase Peters and Austin: Executives may be able to *order* someone to be at work at 8:30 A.M. But they cannot order anyone to perform in an excellent manner—*excellent* meaning courteous, creative, caring, conscientious. Excellence at all levels is a purely voluntary commitment.

Positive reinforcement works by encouraging employees to place more good things on their agenda. Management's contribution to this process is to gently get others to shift their attention in a desirable direction and to pay attention to and acknowledge desirable new activities. Because people repeat those activities for which they have been rewarded, the positively reinforced behavior is repeated more often and comes to occupy a larger share of time and energy. By definition, something (who cares what?) less desirable begins to drop off. But it drops off at the employee's initiative and motivation rather than management's. So the employee doesn't feel "pushed around."

Rewards and praise are more effective leadership tools than are criticism and punishment. No healthy environment, either at work or at home, would have more negative comments than positive ones. If rewards and praise are more effective leadership tools than criticism and punishment, then why do so many executives pay more attention to *mis*behavior than to *good* behavior. Why do they hand out more negative feedback than positive?

Several conditions can contribute to this phenomenon:

- If supervisors have too many people reporting to them, their time may be fully occupied catching and responding to mistakes just to avoid potential disasters. They are just too overloaded to give much attention to positive behavior.

- Some executives have less power to provide rewards than they have to penalize.

- Many executives can more readily identify poor performance than good performance. Criteria for unacceptable work are more clearly defined than criteria for outstanding work. Poor work also affects a group's performance more obviously than does superior work.

- Some executives who value homogeneity and standardization are more likely to disapprove deviations from the norm than they are to approve the exceptional.

WHY SATISFACTION AND DISSATISFACTION ARE NOT OPPOSITES

Partners often ask, "How do I get an employee to do what I want?" Frederick Herzberg[5] responded, with tongue in cheek: "The surest way to get someone to do something is to kick them in the pants." You may know a partner who "motivates" people with a kick in the pants. Some partners also resort to "psychological kicks" by shouting, threatening, or other forms of intimidation.

But what does a kick accomplish? If you kick someone, either physically or psychologically, who is motivated? *You* are motivated, but *the person you kick* only moves! Kicks lead to movement, but not to motivation.

In addition to these negative kicks, there are *positive* kicks, which include rewards, incentives, status, and promotions. For example, you can use a dog biscuit to get a dog to move. But again, in this instance, all you are doing is applying a kick from the front, exerting a pull rather than a push.

Why is it that partners easily recognize that negative kicks are *not* motivation, while most partners think that positive kicks *are* motivation? It is because negative kicks are rape, and positive kicks are seduction.

Why is a kick not motivation? If you kick your dog (from the front or the back), your dog will move. But when you want your dog to move again, what do you have to do? You have to kick it again. Similarly, you can charge a person's battery with money, or praise, or rewards, and then recharge it, and recharge it again. But it is only when people have a generator of their own that we can talk about motivation. Then they need no outside stimulation. They *want* to do it.

So the real question is: How do you install a generator in an employee? That is what motivation—true motivation—is all about.

Movement is caused by fear of punishment or failure to get rewards.

It is typically used in animal training and behavioral modification techniques for humans. However, real motivation is a function of growth from getting intrinsic rewards out of interesting and challenging work.

You may think: What difference does it make? The end result is the same. Though movement and motivation may appear similar, their different dynamics produce vastly different long-term consequences.

Inducing movement emphasizes short-term results and *requires constant reinforcement*. To get a reaction, you must constantly enhance the external rewards. Motivation, however, is based on a person's growth needs. It is an internal engine, and its benefits show up over a long period of time. Because *the ultimate reward in motivation is personal growth*, people don't need to be rewarded constantly.

Herzberg's article also describes his satisfier–dissatisfier theory: Environmental factors such as pay, comfortable surroundings, and understanding supervisors can at best create no dissatisfaction on the job. If these factors are not present, their absence will create job dissatisfaction. In other words, a bad job environment can drive people away. In contrast, what makes people *happy* on the job and truly *motivates* them are the job *content* factors, such as interesting and challenging work and the opportunity for personal growth and achievement. And that's another reason why you need to delegate interesting and challenging work to staff.

Herzberg's motivation theory has been confirmed by many other investigations. *The factors that produce job satisfaction and motivation are separate and distinct from the factors that lead to job dissatisfaction*. Because separate factors produce job satisfaction and job dissatisfaction, it follows that these two feelings are not opposites of each other. "The opposite of job satisfaction is not job dissatisfaction but, rather, *no* job satisfaction; and, similarly, the opposite of job dissatisfaction is not job satisfaction, but *no* job dissatisfaction."

The growth or *motivator* factors intrinsic to the job:

1. A sense of achievement or accomplishment

2. Recognition or feedback

3. Interest in or pleasure from the work itself

4. Responsibility

5. Advancement or promotion

6. Personal growth

Those are what good management, good leadership—and good executives—help create.

The environmental factors that can only avoid dissatisfaction:

1. Company policy and administration

2. Quality of supervision and the relationship with the supervisor

3. Working conditions

4. Salary

Other moderately important environmental factors are camaraderie, enhancement of or interference with personal life, status, and—last of all—security.

The opposite of job satisfaction is not job dissatisfaction but, rather, *no* job satisfaction; and, similarly, the opposite of job dissatisfaction is not job satisfaction, but *no* job dissatisfaction.[6]

To paraphrase Peter Drucker, professionals whose jobs are too small to challenge and test their abilities either leave for a more challenging environment or decline into mediocrity. "Executives everywhere complain that many young men with fire in their bellies turn so soon into burned-out sticks. They have only themselves to blame; they quenched the fire by making the young man's job too small."[7]

Tom Peters and Nancy Austin[8] suggest a few things for you to think about:

- People are people. . . not personnel.

- People like to work. . . help them understand mutual objectives and they will drive themselves to unbelievable accomplishments.

- People have self-development and self-realization needs, and they will commit themselves only to the extent they can see ways to satisfy those needs.

- People work best in an atmosphere that is challenging, invigorating, and fun. . . and rewards should be related as directly as possible to performance.

- When people are in an atmosphere of trust, they will put themselves at risk; only through risk is there growth, reward, self-confidence, and innovation.

So to motivate your employees, create an environment of professional growth, courtesy, challenge, acknowledgment, and winning.

NOTES

1. Philip B. Crosby, *Quality Without Tears*, New York: McGraw-Hill, 1984, p. 15.

2. Thomas Peters and Robert H. Waterman, Jr., *In Search of Excellence: Lessons from America's Best-Run Companies*, New York: Warner Books, 1982, pp. 56–57.

3. Peters and Waterman, pp. 57–58.

4. Peters and Waterman, p. 68.

5. Frederick Herzberg, "One More Time: How Do You Motivate Employees?," *Harvard Business Review*, September–October 1987, pp. 109–120.

6. Herzberg, p. 112.

7. Peter Drucker, *The Effective Executive*, New York: Harper & Row, 1985, p. 83.

8. Tom Peters and Nancy Austin, *A Passion for Excellence*, New York: Warner Books, 1985, p. 241.

14

Manage the People

From grocery chains to steel companies to car dealerships, when I have observed excellence it has always resulted from applying common sense and common courtesy—to one's people and one's customers.

Thomas J. Peters[1]

All the *real* assets of a professional firm go home every night. The people *are* the firm. Their loyalty, productivity, and service-mindedness can make or break you. And when I say "people," I'm not talking about just the partners, or even just the technical staff; I'm talking about *all* the people, but particularly the front line.

Your frontline people include telephone operators, receptionists, secretaries, and even file clerks. Frequently, these are among the firm's least educated, lowest paid, and poorest trained employees. This is dangerous for professional firms because most of your employees interact with clients, and all those employees' language skills and dress are part of the client's experience with your service.

Goods are consumed, services are *experienced.*

David Maister[2]

Machine-produced widgets are of uniform quality, but services involve personal labor, which can vary greatly each time they are performed. All your revenue comes from selling your people's performance, not from selling widgets. Though you may use word processors, computers, and state-of-the-art technology, all the equipment in the world would not earn a nickel without the people. It is the people who produce the results; technology only makes the people more productive.

YOUR "FRONT DOOR" TO THE WORLD

Your receptionist or whoever answers the telephone is your "front door" to the world.

Example:

I once called a firm, had the phone ring forever, and then was answered with, "Smith & Jones, please hold. [Click.]" How would you feel? I know I was a little miffed.

When the receptionist finally came on the line, I said "Mr. Jones please" and was asked "Who's calling?" So I said "David Cottle" and the reply was "[Click.]" Again how would you feel? I wondered whether the receptionist had even heard me, let alone understood me.

Finally I heard "Mr. Jones's office," so I said "Is he in?" and Jones's secretary said "Who's calling?" To me, that question caused two reactions, both of them bad: (1) If the first operator wasn't going to tell Jones's secretary who I was, why did she ask? And (2) does which name I give have any bearing on whether Jones is "in"? If I give the wrong name, will she say Jones is "out"?

Think of this: Probably more than 90 percent of your firm's communications from the outside world come through your receptionist.

I asked partners at a firm retreat that I was facilitating, "Who has the most contact with clients?" After the obvious answers of "the managing partner" or names of active marketing people, they finally realized it was the receptionist. And then I asked them: "Who is the lowest-paid, least-trained, least-experienced, and least-respected person in the firm?" Light bulbs went on over everyone's heads. The firm had been formed by partners from a large, internationally prominent firm, who had pulled out and begun their own practice. They had experienced spectacular growth for its first two years. Lately, their growth had slowed down. When I asked the question about telephone operators, it directed their attention to their receptionist. They had recently hired a new one, and she wasn't very good. Her lack of telephone and people skills had affected the entire firm's client relations and practice development. I am happy to report that after the retreat, they gave the receptionist some training, and they report that she is doing fine.

> **Key Point:** If you get nothing else from this book, get this: Your receptionist (and your telephone operator and secretary if you have separate positions) are your most important salespersons.

Practical Tip:

Invest in training your receptionist and any others who handle client phone calls. Buy cassette programs, send them to seminars, or buy video training programs, but train these key frontline people *first*.

Most partners seriously underestimate both the importance and the complexity of the receptionist position. It's quite common to hire a new receptionist and say something like, "Here's the phone, there's your desk, good luck!" Then, 10 minutes later, your biggest client calls, and the new receptionist asks her or him, "Could you please spell your name"! Don't laugh; it happens.

> **Key Point:** *Never* put a brand-new person on the front desk without thoroughly training the person.

Here's a sample of things your receptionist will learn from a good seminar or cassette program:

- Don't say, "Who's calling?" Do say, "May I ask who's calling?" or "May I tell Ms. Smith who's calling?"—and then *tell* Ms. Smith.

- Don't say, "He hasn't come in yet." Do say, "He's not in his office at the moment."

- Don't say, "I don't know where she is; I saw her just a minute ago." Do say, "She's away from her desk at the moment."

- Don't say, "He left early today." Do say, "He's out of the office until tomorrow."

- Don't say, "She's out sick." Do say, "She's not in the office today."

Your receptionist has to know

- How to answer the telephone

- Names of every person in the firm

- Title and duties of every person

- What to do if he or she doesn't know how to handle an incoming call

- How to handle complaints

- How to handle telephone solicitors

- How to handle emergencies, including every kind of emergency you normally get

- How to handle angry or upset people

- How to transfer calls (lots of different types of equipment are on the market in the wake of telephone deregulation, and every model is different)

- How to screen calls

- Whose calls to screen and whose not to

- The names of very important people (VIPs) who are *always* put through or otherwise given special treatment

- How to take messages

- How to give messages when the firm's people call in, including what to do with the call slip after the message is delivered

- How to respond to conflicting demands from partners or others

- What other duties your receptionist has and how they rank in priority

These are not just nice-to-know things; these are bare essentials to function at minimal efficiency. I'll bet you didn't realize until you read the preceding list just how complicated the job is, did you? Well, that's why I say you should pay your receptionist more than any other administrative person except the firm administrator.

YOUR FRONTLINE MARKETERS

Attracting clients is a traditional marketing function. But *keeping* clients is a function of interactive marketing. The Ace Widgets customer relationship allows well-known techniques of quality control to ensure that the four P's of the product output conform to desired standards. But the Smith & Jones client relationship also involves the three P's of people, procedures, and physical evidence. As we have just illustrated with your front door to the world, two of the three P's involve moments of truth between your clients and your frontline personnel. Here, the external quality standards include courtesy, kindness, warmth, friendliness, and concern—all of which are a direct result of the actions of your frontline people.

> Executives spend more time on managing people and making people decisions than on anything else, and they should.
>
> *Peter Drucker*[3]

The personnel challenge in professional firms is to manage the practice so that clients' moments of truth add to, rather than detract from, the image of high quality. The inherent weakness of firms is that their people are the prime component of their moments of truth. Furthermore, in some firms, the frontline people include nonprofessionals who are among the lowest paid, least trained people—people such as receptionists, technicians, messengers, and office assistants. And even the so-called professionals could frequently use a lesson or two in friendliness and courtesy. The significance of the people to the client's experiences creates a complex management task. You can think of personnel management as a marketing issue when I call it "client satisfaction." Or you could think of personnel as an operations issue when I call it "service quality assurance." But it's the same issue; the people *are* the practice.

Because of the overwhelming importance of interactive marketing in keeping clients coming back for more, one could truly say, "In a professional practice, the same people do the marketing and the production."

Practical Tip:

Track a routine client transaction (say a physical examination for

a doctor, a collection action for an attorney, a tax return for an accountant, or boarding a pet for a veterinarian) from start to finish. List all the times the client comes into contact with your personnel and who the personnel are. Cover all functions—telephone operator, receptionist, delivery, secretary, etc. The typical list will contain 18 to 20 separate moments of truth!

Are you actively managing all these contacts? What additional management of these contacts could you do?

It goes without saying that frontline people should have a certain level of social skill. Unfortunately, it is all too common to have abrasive, arrogant, or even rude people in frontline positions. Albrecht and Zemke call it the "Gravel Gerty syndrome" (females are usually the ones shunted into jobs like these). Gerty has been with the firm for over 20 years and has worked for just about every partner in the place at some time or other. They have passed her around from department to department, and somebody finally has the bright idea, "Let's put her out in the reception area. That way she won't bother anybody." She doesn't bother anybody in the firm, but she plays havoc with the firm's public image. A client or prospect walks into the lobby, wanting to know where to go or whom to visit. Gerty is unfriendly, short-tempered, and irritable. She treats visitors like pests. The partners don't realize it, but they have put her in exactly the position where she can do the most damage.

Little things like how your telephone is answered can make a big difference. However, what Albrecht and Zemke call "smile training" won't do it either. If you believe that your personnel need training in courtesy, or that the Golden Rule applies only with clients, maybe you need to review your recruiting process. A case where an employee— *any* employee in *any* position—lacks the basic social skills is a recruiting problem, not a training problem. Albrecht and Zemke[4] note that frontline people need to know how to handle irate clients. They also should know how much abuse you expect them to tolerate and how to handle a complaint, "but *not*, we contend, how to 'smile' and be civil."

THE IMPORTANCE OF INTERNAL MARKETING

Because your frontline personnel are the link between the firm and the clients, they must satisfy the needs of both of these groups. Sometimes, the firm's expectations and the clients' expectations are inconsistent. Remember that your frontline personnel are the most important factor

in the long-term success of your client service effort. If your personnel are not sold on the quality of service you provide and on the importance of their roles in providing it, they will never sell your clients on it.

Examples:

- Partners at one large firm were expected to cross-sell additional services to clients whom they handled; some partners felt they were pressured to push unneeded services off on the clients. While some clients needed the expanded scope of the firm's services, some did not. Indiscriminate pressure to cross-sell created unwanted stresses on some partners. They were torn between the firm's expectations and their desire to serve their clients' best interests. Part of the problem was that these partners did not know the people in the other departments very well. Yet they were expected to sell these other departments' services to their clients when they had neither knowledge of their associates' competence nor confidence in their associates' skills.

- A CPA firm expects staff members to process as many individual income tax returns as possible, limiting the amount of time spent with each client. The clients, on the other hand, want to take time to review and discuss their tax situation with the staff.

- A veterinarian expects his or her groomer to groom as many animal patients as possible, limiting the amount of time spent with each patient and its client owner. Clients, however, want personal attention from the staff.

Such role conflicts increase job stress and turnover, reduce job satisfaction, and even increase absenteeism in extreme cases. Performance measurements that focus on the client rather than on internal efficiency reduce the conflict. Compensation based on delivered service quality (measured by client satisfaction) is another way to reduce the conflict.

Selling your personnel on the quality of the firm and their importance to the firm is *internal marketing*. Internal marketing consists of marketing your firm to your front line so that you recruit and retain the best possible people and so that they will do the best possible work. The

objective of internal marketing is to develop client-centered, service-minded people.

Internal marketing to your own personnel is a third type of marketing, in addition to traditional marketing (which brings in new clients) and interactive marketing (which keeps existing clients).

Often, your frontline personnel do not consider themselves to be involved in marketing. In fact, many in your front line would recoil at the suggestion that they were part of the firm's marketing. Accordingly, plan training programs carefully. Initially, it is more important to change employee attitudes toward their jobs than to give courses on sales and communication techniques. Such obvious smile training could even have the adverse effect of increasing an already unfavorable attitude toward marketing. Focus your first seminars on client interaction and client satisfaction skills so that participants will realize their important role in client retention.

As a manager, you have three choices:

1. You can hire people with highly developed client relations skills. They are hard to find because they are in great demand. Those who have these people don't want to let them go. And even if you do find some, they cost a lot of money.

2. If you can't find highly skilled people, you can hire people with potential. Then you systematically train them to develop the skills you need. However, these newly skilled people will then become much in demand, so you will have to make them very, very happy at your firm.

3. If you are not willing to do either of the first two, then the third choice is to do without. This limits you to your current size and current skills base.

To survive, a firm must choose one of the first two options.

GETTING EMPLOYEES TO TAKE EMOTIONAL OWNERSHIP OF THE FIRM

An unmotivated work force is a disadvantage in any business, but in a professional firm, where all you really sell is service, and most of your resources for satisfying clients are your personnel, poorly motivated people can kill you. Productivity and quality of work are directly proportional to the degree of self-motivation your personnel have.

When is the last time you washed a rental car? It may seem like a silly question, but if your personnel don't feel emotional ownership of your firm, why should they work to maintain its positive image? There's no ownership if they're only responsible for what happens at their own desk. People need to know how their job fits into the whole firm. And they need to know how the whole firm is doing.

Your personnel will assume responsibility for peak performance only if they have *managerial vision*—that is, if they can see the firm as if they were personally responsible for its success or failure. They can only attain this vision through the experience of participation.

Jan Carlzon,[5] president and CEO (chief executive officer) of Scandinavian Airlines System, turned SAS from a $20 million annual loss to a $54 million annual profit in one year. How? He said that SAS surely could only have succeeded because so many employees were willing to devote extra time and effort to their jobs. "What made them work so wholeheartedly? I think it was because they all understood our goals and strategies. We communicated a vision of what the company could be, and they were willing to take responsibility for making it work."

Questions To Think About:

- How can you expect your personnel to care about how they treat clients if they don't feel that the clients are *their* clients, too?

- How can you expect people to care about meeting your financial goals when you never share financial-planning information with them?

- How can you expect them to worry about profitability on a service to a client when they don't have any idea about the time or budget projected?

- How can you expect them to keep their charged hours up and their write-downs low when you keep their operating statistics a secret?

You've got to trust the people with whom you work. Trust characterizes the attitude of both sides of a good employment relationship.

The question is not, How much information do our personnel want?

It is, How much should you give to them in order to further the firm's own interest? How much information do they need to allow the firm to demand responsible performance, and when should they get it?

> Anyone who is not given information cannot assume responsibility. But anyone who *is* given information cannot avoid assuming it.
>
> *Jan Carlzon*[6]

Making everybody part of the strategic information stream makes everybody feel emotional ownership.

Several of my very successful client firms even give everyone a copy of each year's complete strategic plan—right down to the newest secretary. People who are part of the team, who feel responsible for the firm and for their job, regularly perform better than the rest. If your personnel look upon the firm as theirs, they cannot help but take responsibility for caring for those clients as if they were their own.

If you wonder why your personnel don't take an entrepreneurial interest in the well-being of the firm, think about whether you have ever told them what the well-being of the firm is! If personnel perceive a firm as inefficiently run, it is extremely hard to motivate them to improve their performance. Regardless of wages and working conditions, a work group derives satisfaction from the efficient performance of the tasks for which it was formed. An inefficient firm diminishes the chances of satisfaction for its personnel.

INTERNAL COMPETITION

> We see many evidences of the use of social comparison by the excellent companies. Among them are regular peer reviews . . . ; information made widely available on comparative performance . . . ; and purposefully induced internal competition.
>
> *Peters and Waterman*[7]

People like to evaluate their performance by comparing themselves to others, not by using absolute standards. That's why runners race faster against other runners than against the clock.

One firm just couldn't seem to get chargeable hours up to par. The partners moaned and groaned and established goals for each employee, but nothing worked. Finally they began posting a list of each employee's total and chargeable hours for the month on the bulletin board—in descending order. They didn't make any speeches. They didn't call anybody's attention to it. They just posted the numbers. Wow! Suddenly those people at the bottom of the list started getting more chargeable time. Each month, they wanted to see their names higher on the list.

One of my clients increased *realization* (the percentage of "standard" rates actually billed) by 7 percent in just four months by the simple expedient of passing out each partner's realization numbers each month. Peer pressure did the rest. The same client also developed a list of what they called "underachievers": specific clients who yielded less than a certain percentage of realization. The list was circulated to all partners each month, and partners began to take a great deal of pride in getting clients for whom they were responsible off the list.

What sort of competitive contests or games can you use to stimulate healthy internal competition?

IMPROVING PEOPLE'S PERFORMANCE WITH FEEDBACK

The number one motivator of people is feedback on the results of their efforts. So often, executives simply ignore employees' performance. They don't give negative feedback *or* positive feedback; they just give no feedback at all. This can cause staff, particularly new staff, to feel that no one cares whether they do well. Generally, no response to good performance tends to decrease the chance the good performance will be repeated. After a while, the staff members just slow down to "half-fast" unless they are doing something that is motivating in and of itself.

Feedback can come from clients, from the work itself, or (in the case of new hires) from their supervisor. Negative feedback is better than no feedback at all, but not much better.

How much recognition is enough? If you are like most people, your view of your performance is that you always do more than is required. You always go the extra mile. This seemingly high self-assessment is shared by 90 percent of the working population. And it is, by and large, a correct assessment for most people.

Therefore, it is appropriate to give substantial acknowledgment or recognition for even routine actions—which are usually not so routine—as well as for exceptional accomplishments. Create an environment in which your personnel can achieve/produce/win/grow; identify ways to recognize or acknowledge their achievements.

It is easier for people at *all* levels in the firm, including partners, to do well if they get clear feedback from others on how well they are doing. This is true for all people in all situations, and particularly true for staff.

Feedback generally comes in three forms:

1. *Information*, which is data regarding how the person is doing compared to her or his goals (which may include coaching on how to improve skills)

2. *Positive feedback*, which some people call "applause" or "praise"

3. *Negative feedback*, which some authors call "reprimands"

The *One-Minute Manager*[8] series says "Coach to teach skills, and reprimand to change attitudes." This may be appropriate in some organizations, but I believe that professional practices should only hire people with good attitudes. If you have good executive and leadership skills, those good attitudes will remain good and even improve. If you made a hiring mistake and picked a bad apple with a predominantly bad attitude, show that person the door. However, occasional lapses in attitude can happen even to the most motivated person. All incidents of less-than-optimum behavior are caused either by lack of knowledge or by temporary bad attitude. You can handle either type of incident with good coaching.

Lots of partners give instant feedback when employees are doing poorly. Unfortunately, most partners are not so quick to praise employees when they do well. It is far more important to catch people doing something right than to catch them doing something wrong. Catching someone doing something right puts everyone's attention on the positive, productive aspects of their jobs. When this happens, the negatives tend to reduce by themselves, almost by magic. That doesn't mean that you should *never* criticize; just don't forget to praise.

MAKING A LITTLE PRAISE GO A LONG WAY

When you see people, particularly staff, doing something right, praise them with positive feedback and information. Tell them precisely what they did right. Then watch them light up!

This has a highly beneficial effect on people because it is immediate; they don't have to wait for an annual or semiannual performance review to see how well they are doing. Also, by specifying exactly what someone was doing right, the person knows you are both sincere and informed.

Consistently praise staff and partners when they are doing well, even if other areas of your business are not doing well. In other words, if one of your associates is doing well, praise the associate even if your other areas of responsibility are annoying you. Respond to where the associate is, not just to where you are.

Praising requires more than just saying, "Good job." Here's how to praise:

1. Tell people *ahead of time* that you are going to tell them how they are doing. Otherwise, they may be shocked the first time you notice they did something right, particularly if this is a new habit for you.

2. Praise people immediately; don't wait for their regular performance appraisal.

3. Tell people exactly what they did right—be specific.

4. Tell people how it helps the firm and the other people who work there, as well as, you hope, the client.

5. Encourage them to do more of the same.

You may have heard the old rule, "Always praise in public and criticize in private." Generally this is good advice, but there are two reasons it may not be appropriate:

1. Some people appreciate public praise; some are embarrassed by it. Don't assume that your own preferences are shared by your assistants. Public praise has a beneficial effect on everyone who hears it, but some assistants prefer to be praised privately. Respect their wishes.

2. Also, if you make a habit of *always* praising in public, then every time you call someone into your office and close the door, they—as well as everyone else in the office—will know you are going to reprimand them. So consider doing some of your praising in private.

If you have been in the habit of also criticizing in public, **Stop!**
Some commonly ineffective kinds of praise:

- Too general—Be specific.

- Too little—Some people need it heaped on them, some are satisfied with a word or two, so tailor the amount and intensity of the praise to the person being praised.

- Too late—Respond immediately.

- Mixed with criticism ("Nice job, *but* why didn't you. . .?")—Make your praise unalloyed.

- Phony—Be sincere.

Incidentally, many people have difficulty receiving praise. They just don't know how to handle it at first. This is usually because they have so little practice being praised. Help them perfect this skill by giving them lots of practice!

After a while, people will learn to accept positive feedback from you, from clients, and from the nature of the job itself. They help create their own acknowledgments and develop a momentum of accomplishment.

IMPROVING PEOPLE'S SKILLS

My father used to remind me occasionally that there was a lot of difference between having 15 years of experience and having 1 year of experience 15 times. The difference is the ability to learn lessons from the successes and failures we have been exposed to. Good coaching helps us to turn exposure into experience. Coaching is an investment of expensive management time for the long-run good of the firm and of the "coachee."

The professions, no less than industrial America, find it all too easy to sacrifice the long-term health of their organizations to the cause of short-term profitability. Accordingly, coaching is not recognized and rewarded, and hence it tends to fall to those who find it personally fulfilling or who value the future benefits to the firm more than their own short-term self-interest.

David Maister[9]

What should you do if an assistant is making mistakes? Coach the assistant to improve his or her skills. Mistakes are a learning opportunity, not a chance for the executive to unload hostility onto somebody. Nobody learns except by trying new things and making mistakes.

> Never castigate. Babies learn to walk by falling down. If you beat a baby every time he falls down, he'll never care much for walking.
> My batting average on decisions at Avis was no better than .333. Two out of every three decisions I made were wrong. But my mistakes were discussed openly and most of them corrected with a little help from my friends.
>
> *Robert Townsend*[10]

The better your people are, the more mistakes they will make because they will try more new things. The purpose of coaching is to improve the performance of the coachee. The role of the coach is to help other people to improve their skills. If, at the conclusion of coaching, your assistants have improved their skills, then you have both won. The idea is for both members of the same team to be winners.

Coaching is a mild teaching experience, as distinguished from criticism or a reprimand, which has negative emotional reactions. Coaching requires specific skills to achieve good results for both the executive and the assistant.

In your own mind, differentiate between the person and the problem. The *person* is *not* the problem; the problem is the person's *behavior.* The behavior may be caused by a temporary bad attitude or by ignorance. If the bad attitude is not temporary, get rid of the employee. In either of the cases when you want to keep the person, the person is okay; the less-than-optimum behavior is not.

Remember that you and the assistant almost never see a situation the same way. You can't; you are two different people with two different viewpoints. Here's yet another application of the principle, "Reality is what you can perceive clearly." Stop and think before you coach or criticize. Find out how the other person perceives the issue before you do anything about it. If you identify a problem with the assistant, you cannot get progress or agreement on the solution until the assistant agrees that there *is* a problem. Invest as much time as necessary to agree on what the problem is. Then it's relatively easy to agree on a solution. In fact, many times your assistant will see the solution by the time that you do.

Steps for Coaching

Each coaching opportunity has four or five parts: the event, the effect, your reaction (which is optional), your advice, and a validation of the assistant's worth.

The Event

The event is exactly what happened, or what the problem is. Cover who, what, when, where, how, and why. Be factual and not emotional. Tell the assistant precisely what he or she did wrong. State the specific behavior that was in error and why. Don't be shy; *you are not assigning blame.* This is important enough to repeat: *You are not assigning blame.* After all, the mistake was a lack of knowledge or a temporary lapse of attitude, and your coaching will handle it.

It is essential for you and the assistant to agree on the significant facts. If you don't agree on the facts, you and the assistant have not discussed the situation thoroughly enough to handle it yet. Once you agree on the facts, you can go to step two, which is . . .

The Effect

The effect is the consequence(s) that the event had on the firm, the client, you, the other members of the team, or even the assistant himself or herself. Probably, the assistant doesn't truly understand why his or her behavior was inappropriate; if the person did, she or he would not have done it in the first place. Cover the quantity, quality, time, cost, space or location, and the people affected.

Make the impact real without overwhelming the assistant. Keep a proper perspective. Avoid saying "always" and "never." Remember, your purpose is not to punish but to improve the assistant's performance *in the future.* In most training or coaching situations, the damage will be minimal because you should assign only low-risk tasks to trainees—If you assign high-risk tasks to trainees, you should blame yourself, not the trainee.

Your Reaction

Your reaction is how you feel about the event. Telling the assistant this is optional. Well-motivated people want to do better. Just explaining the event and its effect may send some assistants off on a guilt trip. This is not what you want. You want them charged up to do better, not hanging their heads in shame. Occasionally, you may give your reaction, *if* it will have a *beneficial effect* on the *assistant*, such as when their attitude needs a little upgrading. Giving your reaction means telling the assistant how you are personally affected by the mistake. Also, remember that it's not that bad—After all, you're still alive and in business.

Your Advice

Your advice is your opportunity to improve the assistant's performance in the future. You may suggest changes, establish future policy to cover similar situations, or simply direct the assistant regarding how to handle this kind of situation in the future. Don't dwell in the past by pointing fingers and assigning blame. Instead, help the assistant learn from it so that she or he can do better in the future.

Validation of the Person

Then *remind* the assistant how competent you think he or she usually is. This had better be true or this assistant would not still be working for the firm.

It is very important not to criticize learners. That is too reminiscent of what Blanchard and Johnson[11] call the "leave alone—zap" style of management. "You leave a person alone, expecting good performance from them, and when you don't get it, you zap them." What happens to these unfortunate "zapees" is that they learn to *do as little as possible* to avoid getting zapped. It will immobilize them by making them afraid to do anything. To teach skills, you use coaching.

Tips on Coaching

After you coach a trainee, don't just leave the trainee alone. Observe the trainee's performance, and then either praise the progress or go back to coaching again.

Like applause, an appropriate coaching has a beneficial effect on the employee.

1. Coach assistants as soon as you confirm that they did something wrong. After all, you want inappropriate behavior stopped and the appropriate behavior learned. The best way to do this is to teach it as soon as possible.

2. Specify exactly what the assistants did wrong; they then know you are on top of what they're doing.

3. Do not attack assistants as persons; you only want to improve their behavior. This makes it easier for them to take advice without becoming defensive.

4. Be consistent. Coach assistants whenever they need to improve their skills or judgment.

> **Key Point:** Coaching has no element of blame, so assistants should not feel bad or guilty when you coach them. In fact, if assistants feel bad or guilty when you coach them, you are doing something wrong.

Usually, if you have handled assistants' attitudes by coaching them realistically and if you have not gotten emotional or tried to overwhelm or intimidate them, they will accept full responsibility for the problem and will apologize and offer to make amends if possible. If amends are possible, allow them to do this; if it's too late, it's too late. Either way, if an assistant takes emotional responsibility, say, "I forgive you." Forgiveness is important to people. After all, they have accepted responsibility and tried to make amends and, as far as they are concerned, the scales are balanced again. Your forgiveness allows them to reassume a productive role with their head held high. *When it's over, it's over*, and telling assistants you forgive them allows the incident to be truly over. Don't just forgive assistants in your heart and assume that they will know you don't hold a grudge. Say these *words*: "I forgive you." This may embarrass you, but believe me it will make a big difference in the employee's attitude toward you in the future.

If you can't forgive the assistant, you have not handled the situation correctly. Either you didn't explain the situation adequately to allow the assistant to accept responsibility, or you and the assistant do not agree on the facts. In either case, you had better try to communicate more effectively.

> **Key Point:** When people who are still learning make a mistake, you go back to training or coaching.

Unfortunately, some executives are what Blanchard and Johnson call "gunnysack" discipliners: They store up observations of poor behavior and then when performance review comes or they are angry in general because "the sack is so full," they charge in and "dump everything on the table." They tell people all the things they have done wrong for the past few weeks or months.

It is important to intervene early so you can deal with one bad behavior at a time. This way, the person receiving the discipline is not overwhelmed.

Key Point: If you are in the habit of overwhelming or intimidating your personnel (or your clients), you can bet they will begin to look for another job (or another professional).

You can't straighten teeth with a hammer! Slow, steady influence and strong emphasis on the new ways will eventually have its effect. It takes a fully loaded supertanker several miles to stop or change direction. Some people take almost as much effort.

Winners are easy to supervise. Set a goal with them and they take off. You don't even have to praise them much; they have such a good self-image that they don't need as much praise as more average people do. You also don't have to coach or reset goals very often; winners tend to do it themselves. If they make a mistake, they usually catch it and correct it before anyone else notices.

CALLING A ROSE BY ANY OTHER NAME

What do you call your personnel? W. L. Gore & Associates (maker of Goretex, a synthetic fabric) doesn't have "employees"; it has "associates." Disney has "cast members."

Many winning firms don't have "juniors," they have "staff" or "associates." Incidentally, some of them don't have "professional staff" either; that term implies that support personnel are not professional. And they don't have "clerical staff" either. Instead, they have "technical staff," which *includes* paraprofessionals, and either "support staff" or "office staff" or "administrative staff."

One of my successful CPA firm clients recently changed the name of their paraprofessionals; they now call them "associate accountants." As one of their partners told me, "The paras soak up all the education we can give them, and they ask for more. Most of them are anxious to learn and take on more responsibility."

ENJOYING THE NATIONAL PASTIME: "BOSS WATCHING"

Whether they know it or not, the partners have a dramatic influence on social standards such as language standards, public decorum, interpersonal behavior, and dress. For example: Do romances intrude into the work place? Are there clear rules for people to follow? Are sexist jokes permitted or encouraged? The partners set the tone.

> **Example:** I first entered the profession as an employee of a national firm in Dallas, Texas in the summer of 1964. Like many people then I wore short-sleeved dress shirts because of the heat. After several weeks, I noticed that one of my supervisors, a senior accountant, always wore long-sleeved dress shirts. When I asked why, he replied, "Because I have noticed that all the partners of this firm always wear long-sleeved shirts." He had been more astute than I in watching *his* bosses.

Bosses exert a far more powerful influence in far more ways than they realize. So what kind of role model are you? How about your partners? If you don't like the answers to those questions, you need to have a soul-searching, heart-to-heart talk with yourself or your partners.

NOTES

1. Thomas J. Peters, "Foreword." In Buck Rogers, *The IBM Way*, New York: Harper & Row, 1986, p. xii.
2. David Maister, "Quality Work Doesn't Mean Quality Service," *The American Lawyer*, April 1984, p. 7.
3. Peter Drucker, *The Frontiers of Management*, New York: Harper & Row, 1986, p. 119.
4. K. Albrecht and R Zemke, *Service America!*, Homewood, IL: Dow Jones-Irwin, 1985, p. 111.
5. Jan Carlzon, *Moments of Truth*, Cambridge, MA: Ballinger Publishing, 1987, p. 18.

6. Jan Carlzon, 1987, p. 27.

7. Thomas J. Peters and Robert Waterman, *In Search of Excellence: Lessons from America's Best-Run Companies*, New York: Warner Books, 1982, p. 72.

8. Kenneth Blanchard and Spencer Johnson, *The One Minute Manager*, New York: Berkley Books, 1981, p. 83.

9. David Maister, "How to Build Human Capital," *The American Lawyer*, June 1984, p. 7.

10. Robert Townsend, *Further Up The Organization*, New York: Harper & Row, 1988, p. 141.

11. Blanchard and Johnson, 1981, p. 83.

15

How to Develop a High-Quality Culture in Your Firm

Superior service quality on a sustained basis requires that high-quality become embedded in the firm's culture. And building a client-centered culture for high-quality service requires leadership at the top—from the partners.

American Airlines has had a formal quality program for more than 30 years.[1] The vice president of passenger services makes a weekly presentation to top management on the company's quality performance. Data is collected by a quality consultant who rides the planes to check service. Customers are asked to fill out opinion surveys. The company measures the elapsed time before reservation phones are answered. American has dozens of service standards covering every facet of the operation. Reservation phones should be answered within 20 seconds at least 80 percent of the time; doors should be opened for deplaning within 70 seconds; etc. Employee compensation, including incentives and merit raises, is tied to achieving these standards.

Like American Airlines, a professional service firm should develop a corporate culture devoted to client-centered, high-quality service. Commitment to quality must pervade the firm. It starts at the top, of course, but it cannot end there. Quality happens in the trenches, on the front lines. That's why it's so important to get employees to feel emotional ownership of the firm. In reviewing published case histories of companies known for high-quality service, there is one constant—the *pervasiveness* of quality consciousness in these companies. Here's what you have to do to develop quality consciousness in your firm:

1. Establish high quality standards

2. Hire personnel with the capacity to meet those standards (which is beyond the scope of this book to address)

3. Train your personnel to meet the high quality standards

4. Check to see that they *are* meeting those standards

5. Reward them when they successfully do so

ESTABLISH HIGH QUALITY STANDARDS

Internal quality standards have been well established by the various professional societies and licensing boards. Naturally, you have already established appropriate quality controls in these areas, and your personnel are following them.

However, external quality is both more visible and more important to clients. Unfortunately, most firms have few, if any, standards for external quality. If you want external quality, you need external quality standards and an external quality control program. Therefore, provide meaningful external quality standards so that your personnel will know what you mean by high quality.

Examples:

- Telephone messages returned within 24 hours

- Correspondence typed within *X* hours of being dictated

- Reports reviewed within *X* days of going to the review department

- Documents delivered within *X* days of the information being received

---

Questions To Think About:

- What external quality standards does your firm have?

- What changes, if any, should you make in existing external quality standards?

- What new areas should you cover with quality standards?

- Name five "coffee stain" irritants your firm regularly subjects your clients to. (If you think there aren't any, keep looking; they're there. If you need to, ask your staff or your clients; they know about them. It may be something as obvious as double call screening, or something as subtle as a too-cold reception room.) What "coffee stains" can you clean up?

- What are the top 10 "Kleenex® box" benefits you provide? What additional "Kleenex® box" experiences can you provide?

Practical Tips—Do a check for small signs of courtesy:

- How soon do you answer the telephone?

- Are your lines ever busy? (Remember that even the smallest practice should have four incoming lines.)

- How long are clients placed on hold?

- Does your receptionist offer *every* client a refreshment?

- What is your "thank you" score?

Hold a series of firm meetings, maybe even a retreat to think and talk about clients. Assign certain chapters of this book for everyone to read before the meetings, and brainstorm the concepts in each chapter. Develop nitty-gritty doable standards for every important moment of truth. Don't try to do it at one meeting; Rome wasn't built in a day. Institute only two or three ideas per month. Before you know it, you'll have made some real progress in client satisfaction.

TRAIN PERSONNEL TO MEET THE QUALITY STANDARDS

Development of knowledge and skills is a process, not an event. Regular staff training should continue all the time. Chapter 14 gave you a few pointers on coaching your personnel. Here are a few more things to think about . . . .

Questions To Think About:

- How are you training your support personnel to meet your existing quality standards?

- How should you train your support personnel to meet any changed or new standards?

- How are you training your technical personnel to meet your existing quality standards?

- How should you train your technical personnel to meet any changed or new standards?

Professionals face a tremendous challenge—the need for continuous learning and relearning. A few generations ago, people could assume that what they had learned by the end of their university education would not ever be significantly changed. This was the assumption on which traditional education and apprenticeship were based. Nowadays, however, professionals have to learn new things continuously after graduation, and they frequently have to relearn them. This applies not only in your technical areas but also in management, marketing— and now in client relations.

> The carpenter can still assume, perhaps, that the skills he [or she] acquired as apprentice and journeyman will serve him [or her] forty years later. [Professionals and executives] had better assume that the skills, knowledge, and tools they will have to master and apply fifteen years hence are going to be different and new. Indeed they better assume that fifteen years hence they will be doing new and quite different things, will have new and different goals and, indeed, in many cases, different "careers."
>
> *Peter Drucker*[2]

The goal of training is to prepare people for their next assignment and for future increases in responsibility. This applies to you as well as to your assistants. The training you give your assistants helps them perform their next and future assignments. Some of those assignments will be technical in nature, but as your assistants mature in your profession, their assignments and responsibilities change. Not only will they continue to have technical responsibilities, but they also will have client relations, management, and marketing responsibilities.

Recall your three choices as a manager: (1) Hire people with highly developed skills who are hard to find and in great demand. (2) Hire people with potential, and train them to develop the skills you need. Or (3) do without and limit your firm to its current size and its current skill base. For your firm to survive, it must choose one of the first two options.

Inch by Inch, It's a Cinch

If you wanted to train someone, say, your niece, to drive, you wouldn't start her out in rush-hour traffic on a busy freeway. You would start her on a large, empty parking lot where she couldn't hit anything. You would start out with little goals—start, stop, drive straight—that she could achieve. Gradually, as your student gained skills, you and she would mutually set more demanding goals until finally your niece would be a driver capable of handling situations far more complicated than she would have imagined before her first lesson.

The two most important things in training anybody to become a winner are (1) to help them learn to *do* simple tasks and (2) to gradually move them upward to more complex and more valuable skills. In other words: (1) Get them involved with *doing* the action; let them do it as soon as possible and as much as possible. And (2) approach the development of skills as you would climbing a staircase: one step at a time.

> Put a 5-foot-10-inch person into 6 feet 3 inches of water, and odds are he'll learn to swim. He may sputter and spit a bit, but he can always hop up off the bottom and get air. Put that same person in 7 feet 4 inches of water, and you may have a dead body on your hands.
>
> *Tom Peters*[3]

Sometimes, your personnel will *ask* for 7-feet-4-inch targets. Don't let them do it; you'll be setting them up for a failure. You want to teach people that they are winners and they can succeed, which encourages them to take on more responsibility.

The objective of both training and goal setting is to turn your personnel into confident winners. Set targets that stretch people, but the real

art is in creating targets that are challenging but achievable. The key is
to set the appropriate gradient. You can't climb a staircase to the second
floor in one step, and neither can your assistants. Trying to stride a floor
at a time instead of a step at a time can overwhelm and demoralize the
learner. If you get previously demoralized assistants, you may have to
create two-inch hurdles for them to jump to teach them they can win.

You want to create an atmosphere of degrees of winning, rather than
of winners and losers. Punishment and other negative outcomes such
as embarrassment or ridicule are a futile strategy in general, but particularly when new behaviors are required. Punishment drives people to
hide and be more averse to risk and trying new things.

Training your personnel to higher and more valuable skills pays off
in several ways. First, it helps keep them motivated because they keep
growing professionally. Second, clients like to see their professionals'
staff get ahead. Finally, you can eventually delegate some of your work
to better-trained staff and be confident that it will be done right.

USE THE MAGIC OF LEVERAGE

In the same way that leverage financing—borrowing money—can allow
a business to produce more with the same equity capital, so too can
delegating service tasks magnify the productivity of an individual partner.

The high income levels you expect from being a partner come only
in part from being able to charge high rates for your personal time. In
the real world, not all work that partners do is at the partner level. This
means that a lot of "pick-and-shovel" work needs to be done. If partners
have to do this lower-level work, clients are not willing to pay partner
rates; write-downs occur. Assistants can do this pick-and-shovel work
and may find it professionally challenging when a partner would be
bored to tears with it. Such work is part of the apprenticeship process
whereby associates acquire higher technical skills based in part on this
pick-and-shovel experience.

A partner's high income is also derived from the firm's ability to
leverage its partners' skills with the efforts of less-costly people. Often,
the firm can realize surplus value by using associates to do higher-level
work under a partner's supervision, though the associates, acting inde-
pendently, could not bill out their efforts at the rates your firm can
charge. They can only get these higher rates because associates' efforts
are performed under the guidance of the partners. By the same token,

however, for a typical client, all the work needed is not partner-level work. A client for whom your firm works 1000 hours a year may, depending on the profession, have only from 50 to 400 hours of true partner-level work in those 1000 hours. So the partners must do the partner-level work and delegate the staff-level work to associates.

Another benefit of delegation is that you can deliver at least the same quality of service with a higher proportion of associates to partners.

MONITOR THE QUALITY OF PERFORMANCE

This task is the toughest one of all—particularly for something as subjective as client satisfaction. Other areas are much easier to measure: compliance with technical standards, chargeable hours, write-ups, write-downs, hours managed, revenues managed, and so forth. Excellent firms measure performance in these traditional *hard number* (easily measured in quantitative terms) areas and keep score on each person—including partners. However, to be truly excellent, you must also go beyond that: Keep regular tracking studies of client perceptions. An annual perception survey of both clients and referral sources lets you know how well you are doing and how well each of your key personnel is doing.

Monitor employee attitudes, as well as client and referral-source attitudes. Ask employees,

1. "What is the biggest problem you face in trying to deliver quality service day in and day out?"

2. "If you were the managing partner and could make only one change to improve quality, what would it be?"

3. "Is there anything else we should do to make it easier for you to serve our clients?"

4. "Is there anything we should *stop* doing that hinders your efforts to serve our clients?"

When consulting with professional firms, I find that some of my best recommendations are already foreseen by staff. When I interview them, they really do know what's going on in the trenches. They will tell *you* if you will ask—and listen.

Most positions have some measurable result of doing the requisite work. For technical staff, it may be chargeable hours; for typists, it might be pages typed; for file clerks, it is files retrieved and refiled, and so forth. You might look upon these measurable results as the "products" of that particular post. Consider formulating appropriate statistics for every post in your firm so that you and the people in those positions can keep tabs on how well they are doing.

If you don't know how to measure the performance of, say, a receptionist, why not ask her or him? The same could be said of clerical and other support personnel. Don't just omit them from your performance standards because their work may be hard to measure. The fact that it may be hard to measure makes it even more important that you do measure it. How else will you know if they are doing the job?

Questions To Think About:

- How do you currently monitor the quality of performance?
- Should you consider a client feedback program?
- Should you consider a client perception survey?

REWARD OUTSTANDING PERFORMANCE

This means that you must have measurable standards. Your reward system should be timely, meaningful, accurate, simple, and fair. It should both anticipate meeting normal standards and reward exceptional performance.

Rewards can be money, recognition, and/or career advancement. As long as you pay adequate salaries and bonuses, money is not a particularly good reward; it's not personal enough. Consider awarding plaques, citations, or medals—with appropriate ceremony and applause, of course. It's the ceremony that makes the awards special.

Tangible recognition doesn't have to be a big deal to be effective. Dinner and a show for two is certainly a suitable way to show appreciation. IBM calls it "A Night on the Town." Many companies specially recognize an employee each month, demonstrating the same type of recognition. One firm hung a brass bell in the hall; every time a new client was brought in, the bell was rung so that everyone in the office would be aware of it.

An occasional big splash can do wonders. Buck Rogers[4] related one such episode: At a company affair, a suitcase filled with dollar bills was dumped on the table as the master of ceremonies invited the recipients to "Please come here and pick up your money!" Then the emcee explained what each person did to earn the award. Rogers: "Any size business can give a plaque, a television set or a check to express gratitude for extraordinary behind-the-scenes sales support. . . . Nothing beats praise when it's deserved."

One accounting firm had a particular employee who had done a remarkably outstanding job for several months. The managing partner decided to give him a large bonus, but the managing partner wanted to have a dramatic effect on the rest of the firm also. At a meeting of the entire staff, the managing partner opened a briefcase and dumped several thousand dollars in currency in the middle of the conference room table and said, "This is for you for the great job you did on, etc., etc." *What* the employee was being recognized for is not important. What is important is the *manner* with which he was recognized. Imagine the impact this dramatic gesture had, not only on the employee but also on the other staff!

Questions To Think About:

- How do you currently recognize outstanding performance?

- How should you recognize outstanding performance in the future?

- What appropriate awards could you institute in the firm?

NOTES

1. Leonard L. Berry, Valarie A. Zeithaml, and A. Parasuraman, "Quality Counts in Services, Too," *Business Horizons,* May/June 1985, p. 51.

2. Peter Drucker, *Innovation and Entrepreneurship,* New York: Harper & Row, 1985, p. 264.

3. Tom Peters, *Thriving on Chaos,* New York: Alfred A. Knopf, 1987, p. 498.

4. Buck Rogers, *The IBM Way,* New York: Harper & Row, 1986, p. 50.

16

Stay in Touch

Unique to intangible products is that the customer is seldom
aware when he's being served well. . . . Only when he doesn't get
what he bargained for does he become aware of *what* he bargained
for. Only on dissatisfaction does he dwell. Satisfaction is, as it
should be, mute.

Theodore Levitt[1]

Let's see how that works in real life: How good is the service at Federal
Express, IBM, or Walt Disney World? You probably said that their
service is terrific. Okay, how good is the service at the post office or
your local utility company? You probably rated them much lower.

Actually, both groups give excellent service for a very reasonable
price. How else could you send a message thousands of miles for only
a few cents? Or flip a switch anytime, day or night, and get unlimited
electric power?

The reason organizations like Federal Express, IBM, and Disney have
an excellent service reputation is that *they constantly remind their
customers of their great service.* The Postal Service and utility companies don't remind their customers that they are being well served. As
a result, we all take good postal or utility service for granted. We only
think about these services when a package is delayed or the lights go
out. When they do a good job, we don't notice; when they do a bad job,
we do notice.

Regularly communicate to clients what you are doing for them. Make your invisible, intangible services as visible as possible. As Levitt said, clients are seldom aware when they are being served well. In fact, they usually don't know what they're getting until they don't get it. Only when they don't get what they bargained for do they become aware of what they did bargain for. Only on dissatisfaction do they dwell; satisfaction is mute.

Reality is what you can perceive clearly. So it's not the quality of service that you give but the quality of service that clients perceive clearly that keeps them coming back.

In keeping clients, it is very important to regularly remind them what a great job you are doing. If you don't remind them, they won't know. They will only notice when they don't get what they wanted. And that's all that counts unless, in the meantime, you have regularly and persuasively reminded them of what you have been doing for them all along. You know the old saying: "What have you done for me lately?" If clients remember what you have done for them lately, your occasional failures fade in relative importance.

> **Example:** When an insurance prospect is heavily romanced and finally sold a policy, the subsequent silence and inattention can be deafening. Most clients seldom recall what kind of life insurance package they bought and often forget the name of the agent and issuing company. A year later they are reminded of this inattention by receiving a premium notice. Is it any wonder the lapse rate is so high?

Once you have cemented a relationship, you have an equity in the client. To help keep the client, continue to re-create the relationship lest it decline and evaporate. There are innumerable ways to do this, and many of them can be systematized. Your best communications medium is in person, but this is also the most costly. Next best is the telephone. Third best is a personal letter, and worst is a form letter.

Practical Tips:

- Periodic letters and telephone calls remind the client of how well things are going, and they are surprisingly inexpensive.

- Quarterly newsletters keep your name and services in front of clients, prospects, and referral sources.

- Nonbusiness socializing has great value.

- When you see a newspaper or magazine article that would be of interest to a major or key client or to several regular clients, send a copy of it to them, along with a personal note. This takes 30 seconds of your time because your secretary can do 95 percent of the work.

- Become a resource to other people, such as introducing clients to others whom you know can be mutually helpful to your clients.

Staying in touch is another area where you can train your front line how to remind clients of the great job you are doing.

"TANGIBILIZE" YOUR SERVICES

This chapter has suggested several ways to reinforce in your clients' minds that you are there and ready to help them. You remind them you are thinking of them. In essence, your communication "tangibilizes" (makes tangible) your service.

Here's an example of tangibilized service:

Take . . . the instructive case of house insulation, a necessity most homeowners approach with understandable apprehension. Suppose you call two companies to bid on your house. The first insulation installer arrives in his car. After pacing once around the house with measured self-assurance and making quick calculations on the back of an envelope, he confidently quotes $2,400 for six-inch fiberglass, total satisfaction guaranteed. Another drives up in a clean white truck with clipboard in hand. He scrupulously measures the house dimensions, counts the windows, crawls the attic, records from a source book the area's seasonal temperature ranges and wind velocities. He asks a host of questions, meanwhile recording everything with obvious diligence. He then promises to return in three days, which he does, with a typed proposal for six-inch fiberglass insulation at $2,600, total satisfaction guaranteed. From which will you buy?

The latter has tangibilized the intangible, made a promise into a credible expectation.[2]

House insulation may be tangible in the store, but it is strictly invisible inside your walls. By taking the invisible product and "making a production" out of it, the second supplier added value to what is essentially an intangible.

Examples:

- Surveyors tangibilize their service by leaving surveyors' flags and bright orange paint spots on curbs and sidewalks, to remind the client they have been there.

- Some auto repair garages return the old, worn-out part to their customers to demonstrate that the part needed to be replaced.

- Anesthesiologists, who need never be seen by their patients, usually visit the patient before and after the operation so that they are perceived as real people to the patient when they present the bill.

- Savvy accountants tangibilize their tax advice by writing a lengthy letter full of citations and documented research to add value to their recommendation.

- Lawyers can send copies of depositions, letters, petitions, and so forth that they prepare for their clients. They may have no practical value for the client, but they tangibilize the service.

Are there any places in your practice you could tangibilize your service? Have a brainstorming session at your next staff meeting.

FIRE ALARMS AND SMOKE ALARMS IN CLIENT RELATIONS

The best quality control you can personally have for your client relations is to simply observe your clients as you are serving them and as they leave your office, or as you leave theirs. As Yogi Berra said: "You can observe a lot by just watching." Does your client look like the face in Figure 13?

Is your client's face all smiles, bright and shiny? If so, your client relationship is in good shape. Here are some good indicators of a happy client:

- Client smiles when leaving your office

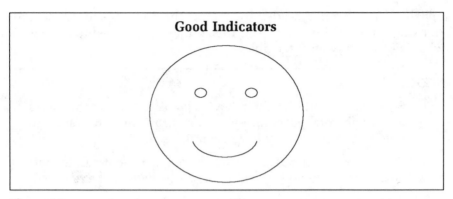

Figure 13

- Client is cheerful to you and your personnel
- Client comes to you for advice on other matters
- Client pays your fee promptly and willingly
- Client responds to your requests for information and cooperation quickly and easily
- Client recommends you to others
- Other personnel in client's organization show these good indicators.

Or does your client or your client's other personnel look like the face in Figure 14? Do your clients look like they had just sucked on a lemon

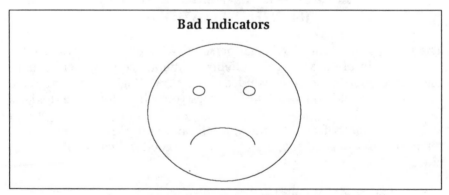

Figure 14

when you show up or when they leave your office? Those bad indicators mean that your client relationship is in danger. Take the preceding
list of good indicators, and turn them "inside-out," and you'll have a list
of the bad indicators.

Key Point: Bad indicators are a fire alarm: They mean you are
about to be fired!

Good indicators and bad indicators are simple once you know what
to look for; the problem arises when your client's face looks like the face
in Figure 15.

These clients have mixed indicators. Those are the clients you have
to watch out for. When someone asks them who their accountant or
lawyer or dentist or doctor is, they pause for a long time as if they don't
want to say anything. Finally, they look at the floor or the ceiling—
anywhere but in the prospect's eye—and say your name really quietly.

There went your referral! You have just been "damned with faint
praise." Your client's body language told the prospect: "Well, I use this
guy (or gal), but I really don't recommend her or him; I'm just too lazy
to fire him or her and break in someone else." Having clients like this
dirties your field and makes your other marketing efforts fruitless.
Here's why:

If the prospect had not asked your client for a referral, you would
have had a chance to get the prospect through your regular marketing
program. The prospect might have seen your sign or found you in the
Yellow Pages or even have asked a different client with a happy face.

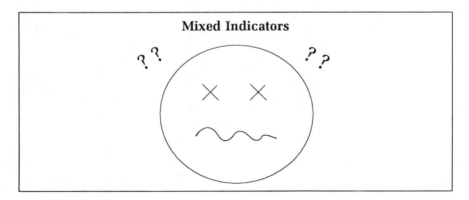

Figure 15

But the prospect didn't; he or she asked a confused client. Now the confused client has given the person your name in such a way that, even if the person hears of you through other marketing channels, he or she would never think of using you.

Frightening, isn't it?

> **Key Point:** A confused client can "vaccinate" prospects against your other marketing efforts.

So stay in touch with your clients and watch their indicators. When you see mixed indicators, it's a "smoke alarm." Part of the problem with bad and mixed indicators is that you don't always see them. This is yet another area where you can train your staff to be observant and report to you on the state of the client relationship.

NOTES

1.   Theodore Levitt, *The Marketing Imagination*, New York: Free Press, 1986, pp. 104–105.
2.   Levitt, p. 108.

17

How to Turn Complaints into Increased Client Loyalty

Have you ever had problems trying to get the IRS or another bureaucracy to resolve a problem? Well, clients have had similar situations. Most of the time, when they have a complaint with almost any other institution, such as banks, credit card companies, department stores, etc., they have experienced so much frustration that they usually expect the worst. Because of those other bad experiences, clients who have problems come to you with both a high level of frustration and a low expectation of satisfaction. That may seem like bad news, but it is actually good news for you: If you can perform well, you will look really good by comparison. Because their expectations are probably very low, it stands to reason that it should be relatively easy for you to exceed those expectations and create a very favorable experience for the client.

COMPLAINTS: DISEASE OR OPPORTUNITY?

When routine service becomes nonroutine—when something goes wrong—the client's sense of frustration is probably high, and his or her expectations for quick or easy satisfaction are probably low. In short, the conditions are ripe for you to *exceed* the client's expectations. But it won't be easy. For one thing, you're not starting out even because the client is unhappy. Your job from the beginning is to come from behind.

243

Examples:

- To paraphrase Peters and Austin,[1] talk to 10 slavishly devoted IBM customers and, surprisingly, you may hear about nothing but problems. *"But,* they always added that whenever a problem had arisen, fifteen IBM people—eleven of them by parachute—had descended on them within three hours. And they always got the machine up just as the first streak of dawn was about to mark the sky. IBM doesn't want to sell you a lemon, for sure, but if they do, they make darned sure you know they are very, very sorry."

- Peters and Austin[2] also report that a senior officer of Johnson & Johnson, the multi-billion-dollar pharmaceutical company, had bought an analytical instrument from a fine company a dozen years before they interviewed him. A couple of months after buying it, he had trouble with a $3 component. Here's how the Johnson & Johnson officer reported the seller's response: "First, they mustered their top engineers to try and prove it was my fault, and that I abused the part and busted it. They were unconscionably tardy in answering my correspondence. They were actually rude over the phone on more than one occasion. Today, fully a dozen years later, I still tell my people, 'Don't buy equipment from those guys.'" Sure, it's irrational, but *feelings are facts.* And *perception is reality.*

- I know of a situation in which a multi-billion-dollar international company had a worldwide contract with a major hotel chain for their traveling personnel. The contract involved thousands of room-nights in their hotels every year and hundreds of thousands of dollars of business. One night, an executive's flight was delayed and he didn't arrive until after midnight. His "guaranteed room" had been sold. The next day, he cancelled his company's contract.

These examples show the benefits of handling complaints well and the drawbacks of handling them badly.

There are two common views of complaints: (1) The more common view is that complaints are a disease to be avoided at all costs. People, firms, and companies holding this view *never* do anything wrong. They *never* make mistakes. And if by some chance anything ever accidentally goes wrong, it is *not their fault.* It is always someone else's responsibility. Witness the illustration of the Johnson & Johnson supplier.

The other view is that a complaint is a *golden opportunity*. For example, IBM sees a complaint as an opportunity to really turn customers on, to make them lifelong friends. Additionally, if you view the complaint in this way, you may even learn something from handling the complaint to help you improve the product or service in the future. In fact, complaints will tell you much the same things that a paid consultant would tell you.

A study by Technical Assistance Research Programs revealed these facts: Twenty-six of every twenty-seven customers who have a bad experience with you fail to report it. The principal reason is not surprising: They expect no satisfaction if they do bug you. The scary part comes next—some 91 percent of those who complain won't come back. Scarier yet, the statistic on dropouts holds as true for $1,000 purchases as for $1.79 ones. And perhaps worst of all, the average person who has been burned tells nine to ten colleagues; 13 percent of the malcontents will spread the bad news to twenty or more people.

There is some hope. The data show that, depending on the industry, you can get 82 to 95 percent of these customers back, if you resolve the complaint in a timely and thoughtful fashion. Other studies are even more optimistic. *A well-handled problem usually breeds more loyalty than you had before the negative incident.*

Tom Peters[3]

Interestingly, the reasons for liking or disliking a company rarely have to do with the product or price. The good or bad experience is almost always related directly to an experience with people, either their attitude or their service. People do business where they are treated well. Strangely, they remember where they were *not* treated well much better than where they were.

Professional firms that are great at problem resolution, who are accessible and responsive with speed, courtesy, and competence, are far more likely to repair the damage done to their quality reputations than those that take a casual "we'll get to it when we can" attitude.

Every client (or former client) with a complaint has 10 friends (or 100) who will hear about it. And half of them will tell *their* friends. It seems as though the smallest dissatisfied client always lives next door to the owner of the company you have been trying for years to get as a client.

Even a big foul-up can turn into a positive experience for the client:

Just call the client back and say you're sorry! Amazingly, a lot of the time that's all you need to do!

ATTITUDE, ATTITUDE, ATTITUDE

Most people are persuaded more by attitude than by logic. This is because most people are strongly influenced by their emotions, and emotions are contagious. Complainers will tend to adopt the same emotional attitude that you have. If you get mad, they'll get mad. If they're mad when they call and you are friendly, they'll tend to get friendly, too.

Let's look at the difference a negative or positive attitude can make. Specifically, let's look at the difference *as perceived by the client* between *willingness* to solve a problem and *ability* to solve a problem.

One research study reported the example of a male participant in a banking services focus group who described the frustration he felt when his bank would not cash his payroll check from a nationally known employer because it was postdated by one day. When someone else in the group pointed out that legal constraints prevented the bank from cashing his check, he responded, "Well, nobody *in the bank* explained that to me!"[4] Because he received no explanation in the bank, this man perceived the bank as unwilling, rather than unable, to cash the check. This resulted in an opinion that the bank's service was of poor quality because it was not able to meet his expectations. (Please refer to the "willingness matrix" in Figure 16.)

1. Willing and Able

Best of all, clients obviously like to deal with people who are both willing and able to solve their problem. You handle any complaint or client request with speed and care. No problem.

Practical Tip:

When handling a problem, assure clients you are helping them *willingly*, not grudgingly. Say things like: "Thanks for calling this to my attention," or "I'm glad I found out about this situation; this way I can take steps to make sure it doesn't happen to other clients, too. Thanks for telling me."

The "Willingness" Matrix		
	Unwilling	Willing
Able	3	1
Unable	4	2

Figure 16

2. Willing and Unable

But what happens when you get a request for something you cannot do? You simply cannot deliver what the client wants.

Examples:

- A client asks you to come to a meeting on short notice when you have another appointment.

- A client has an emergency, and your secretary doesn't know where you are to get a message to you.

- A patient has an incurable disease; as the doctor, you're *willing* to help but *unable to do so.*

From the client's viewpoint, the next best thing to "willing and able" is to be at least *willing* to help even if you are *unable.* Having "your heart in the right place" is worth points, even if you can't perform. This is another example of external quality overcoming temporary lapses in internal quality.

In such cases, all you can do is sympathize. But *don't underestimate the value of sympathy to a client.* I once had a client who sold a partnership interest with a negative tax basis. The client almost gave it away and had to pay tax on the negative basis. He complained loud and long about the unfairness of his having to pay tax on a phantom gain when he had not received any money. I couldn't help him, so I sympa-

thized. Once he grasped the situation and felt my sympathy, he became
a loyal client again.

Practical Tip:

Don't tell clients what you cannot do; tell them what you *can* do.
If they want you to do something beyond your power, don't let
their attention remain on your failure to help. If there is anything,
no matter how small, you can do, offer to do it. For example:
"Sally, I'm sorry I can't meet with you at 2:00 this afternoon. How
about 5:30? Or we could meet at 7:00 tomorrow morning for
breakfast."

---

3. Able but Unwilling

People are extremely frustrated by service people who are *able* to help
(or who seem to be able to help) but are *unwilling*.

Example: Remember the bank that wouldn't cash the customer's
postdated payroll check? The customer had the check; the bank
had the money. The customer perceived that the bank was able but
unwilling to help him when in fact the bank was unable to solve
his problem. What could have been a positive moment of truth
with the bank (or a least a neutral one) turned into a negative
experience. The bank got a failing grade on the customer's report
card.

Questions To Think About:

- Have you ever waited at a sales counter in a store while a
  salesclerk was busy with a personal telephone call?

- What was your reaction?

- How did you feel about the salesclerk?

- How did you feel about the store?

- Do you have any similar situations in your dealings ˜with
  clients?

Before you answer the last question with "no," think a minute. Have you ever taken a telephone call from a second client when you were still in a meeting with the first client? Doing this is like letting the client who telephoned "cut in line" in front of the client who is in your office. Has your receptionist kept a client waiting to be announced while the receptionist finished what was obviously a personal telephone call?

The only hope people have when confronted by an "able but unwilling" situation is if they can just convince the service provider to be *willing* to help, then they will be serviced.

You may believe that your clients would never run into an "able but unwilling" situation in your firm. You may believe that your clients would never perceive you as being unwilling to help them. But let's look back at my client who sold the partnership interest and owed tax on the negative basis. At first, he thought I was *able* to report no gain on the sale but was *unwilling* to do so. This also affected his evaluation of my reliability. First, I had to carefully explain the "why" so the client could see that both he and I had no choice. In other words, I had to convince the client of my *inability* to report the sale at no gain. Then the client could accept that I was *willing* to help but *unable to do so.*

4. Unwilling and Unable

The least desirable professional is perceived as both unwilling and unable to provide a service to the client. The attitude seems to say, "I can't help you, but even if I could, I wouldn't." Assiduously avoid having such an employee, and, if you find one, rapidly ensure that the person becomes a former employee. Make *sure* your clients understand that you are always *willing* to help them, even when you are unable to do so.

WHAT DO COMPLAINERS WANT ANYWAY?

People who write or call with complaints want someone to listen, sympathize, apologize, and, if indicated, correct the matter. And the higher up their complaint is handled, the quicker their fire goes out.

Robert Townsend[5]

Here are a few reasons people complain:

- They didn't get what they expected. You promised them something (or they thought you promised them, which is the same thing) and they didn't get it. It might be as simple as a call-back you didn't make, or a copy of a document you didn't send.

- Somebody was rude on the phone or in person. Obviously it wasn't you (I hope), or the client wouldn't have told you; the client would just have faded away, never to be heard from again. But it might have been one of your associates.

- The client feels that no one made an effort to serve her or him. The client feels that your firm is indifferent to his or her needs. The client may have been ignored, unacknowledged, or unappreciated.

- No one is listening to the client's concern.

- Frontline people project a can't-do or other negative attitude.

Listen—Really Listen

The first problem most complainers have is that nobody really *listens* to them. We all have something to say, and we keep searching for someone to listen. This is especially true when a person has a complaint.

> **Key Point:** The number one thing complainers want is to tell someone about it. And they will.

A complainer is carrying around a 100-pound rock, looking for someplace to unload it. If you won't take it, they'll chip off little pieces and hand some to everyone they meet. Or they'll dump the whole thing with a complaint to your state regulatory board. People with complaints will *always* tell *someone* about it. They have to, or they'll explode. Do you want them to tell *you* or to tell their next-door neighbor and anyone else who will listen? Obviously, you want them to tell you so that they will not feel that they need to tell their neighbor.

Rule number one: *Listen sympathetically to the complaint.* Listen to the whole complaint. Do not interrupt except maybe for clarification, and even getting clarification is not a good idea until the client finishes his or her narrative. Do not make excuses or try to answer the client until he or she finishes saying *everything*.

Caution: It's tempting to think that *listening* means waiting for your turn to talk. However, if you are just waiting for your turn, you lose.

Hear the complainer out completely without interrupting. If you are just waiting for the caller to pause for breath so you can jump in with your side of the story, turn the client over to someone else and hope that he or she can keep the client, because you really don't care about the client; you just care about your ego.

Show Understanding and Concern

Rule number two: *Show understanding and concern.* Repeat back your understanding of what happened from the client's viewpoint. Make sure you can repeat the essential facts to the client's satisfaction before proceeding further. Until you are on the client's wavelength, it is impossible for you to help her or him unless you happen to do the right thing by coincidence. Don't take the chance; make sure you can repeat back the facts as the client sees them. This will also help demonstrate that you understand how important this event was to the client and that you are concerned for the client's well-being.

Practical Tip:

Don't use the word "problem" to describe the event. Saying "problem" sometimes creates one where it didn't exist previously. The client may not have thought he or she had a problem until we named it as such. Instead, say, "As I understand the situation, here is what happened—[describe]. Is that correct?" If it is not correct *from the client's viewpoint*, clear up the point of ambiguity, and try again. Keep repeating back your understanding until the client fully understands and confirms that you have duplicated his or her concern.

If this is a serious matter, you may want to demonstrate your concern further by stating your intention to help. "I'm glad you called this to my attention; I think I can help you." This tells callers that you are on their side and are working with them rather than against them.

Don't blame someone else in the firm. How many times have you heard someone say, "Oh, it's the people in accounts receivable. They don't know what they're doing up there." Remember that you represent the firm—the entire firm. If something goes wrong, don't make it worse by making part of your firm look incompetent.

Don't become defensive; usually, clients aren't blaming you personally. And even if they are, they *think* they have good reason. The client may not always be right, but the client is always the client.

Before proceeding to the solution, ask, "Is there anything else I need to know?" This question is designed to allow clients to vent any remaining frustration and to give them one more chance to communicate fully with you.

Agree on a Solution

Rule number three: *Mutually agree on a solution*. Your attitude here is to put yourself and your clients on the same side: You and they against the problem, not you against them. Sometimes, the solution is obvious once you understand the client's viewpoint. But sometimes clients have difficulty communicating exactly what the problem is or what they expect you to do about it. If the solution is not obvious, discuss the situation with the client and evaluate the advantages and disadvantages of several solutions.

Occasionally, you might even simply ask, "What can I do to make this right with you?" Do they want the service redone, a fee reduction, an apology, or something else?

> **Caution:** Be *very* careful about granting fee reductions because you might inadvertently train clients that you will reduce your fees if they complain. This is a destructive game that you cannot win and that will eventually destroy most client relationships. My general advice is to **never cut a fee!** Some clients will try to dicker over your fee no matter how much or how little it is. Once you establish the precedent of surrendering your fee, you have ruined them forever as good clients. They will come back again and again indefinitely for fee concessions. You won't look very professional.

Practical Tips:

- Don't explain how the mistake happened. Usually, the client doesn't want to hear it, and it can sound like a justification. The exception to this is when the error is *clearly* the client's fault, in which case you must show extreme tact.

- Say what you can do, not what you can't.

- Don't say, "You have to —." People react by thinking, "No, I don't."

- Don't say, "I'll try." You really won't. Either commit to doing something or don't. "I'll try" as a social lie is a killer in a business setting because when you don't do what you say, you will look like a failure.

- Don't say you'll do something "as soon as possible." That's too vague. Say *when* you will call back, or whatever else you intend to do, and then do it. To the client, "as soon as possible" may mean "in the next 10 minutes"; to you, it may mean "within 24 hours." There is too much room for misunderstanding.

- Keep your own attention and the client's in the present and future, not the past. You can't do anything about the past, but you can do something now about the future. So don't say, "Why didn't you —?" It's too late for that.

If the client suggests something minor and easily accomplished, don't be too quick to say "Is that all? Of course we can do that." The client may undervalue your response if you grant it too quickly. I'm not saying to negotiate with the client, and I'm not saying to argue with the client. I'm saying that you should pause and let the client know you are thinking about what he or she said. This complaint is important to the client, and you want her or him to know that it is important to you, too. You might say, "If I understand you correctly, you want us to —. Is that correct? . . . And if we —, you will be happy?" Then say, "I certainly appreciate that you are being reasonable about this. If I were you, I would feel the same way. I will be happy to —. Again, I appreciate your calling this to my attention."

Follow Through and Follow Up

Rule number four: *Follow through.* Do what you say you will do. Make it go right. Either do it personally or have it done under your direct personal supervision. We're talking about the client relationship here, and it is your responsibility to make it go right. Reliability is even more critical here than in the normal situation. The client is already dissatisfied when he or she calls, so you are starting in the hole and have to work your way uphill. Don't promise more than you can deliver, but deliver what you promise.

Rule number five: *Follow up*. Call clients back, and ask them how they feel about your firm now. Are they satisfied? Is there anything else you need to do to make them happy with your service? Don't be afraid to ask for more business. Your relationship should now be stronger than ever.

Learn from Your Mistakes

Rule number six: *Learn from your mistakes*. After handling any complaint, always ask yourself two questions: (1) What would have prevented this problem? (2) What change should I make in our operations to ensure that this doesn't happen to someone else?

By the way, nobody wins them all. Some people just like to be mad. I discuss these unreasonable people a little later in this chapter. Learn to accept defeat philosophically when you lose one.

LISTEN, LISTEN, LISTEN

It is important for the managing partner to get information about complaints. Norman Rachlin, the managing partner of Rachlin & Cohen in Miami, sends a personal letter of welcome to each new client. He closes each letter with "We at Rachlin & Cohen welcome you as a client, and we hope that we will fulfill your expectations. Do not hesitate to contact me directly if you should find we are falling short of the mark."

If necessary, *beg* for complaints. They are there whether you hear them or not. Better your clients complain to you than to their neighbors.

Also, put your best people into problem resolution, not your worst.

Questions To Think About:

- How easy do you make it for your clients to complain?

- Do your clients know how to go about complaining?

- What is your exact method of responding to a complaint?

- Do partners get involved in handling client complaints?

- What evidences of personal concern does the client receive?

- How do your clients perceive your response to their complaints?

- Are you a fanatic about complaints?

- Are any of your competitors better about handling complaints?

HOW TO HANDLE UNREASONABLE CLIENTS

In handling a normal complaint, you only have one assignment: Solve the client's problem. In handling an unreasonable person, you have two assignments: Handle the client's emotions, and then solve the problem. Therefore, your first goal in handling an unreasonable person is to get the person to be reasonable.

Have you ever told an angry or upset person to calm down? Did it work? Of course not. You can't tell upset or unreasonable people, "Be reasonable" because this implies that they are being *un*reasonable. And even the most unreasonable people *think* that they are being very reasonable. Your goal is to discover the reason. You do it by asking questions and listening very carefully to the answers. Use questions such as, "What happened to make you feel this way?" "What do you think caused that?"

Often unreasonable callers are angry. An important fact to remember is that angry people don't *think*; they *feel*. When people have a lowered (i.e., more depressed) emotional tone, their ability to reason and to respond to reason is decreased proportionately. Reason is very high-toned (i.e., up beat); anger and other low-toned emotions detract from the ability to reason.

> **Key Point:** You cannot reason with an angry person.

The big danger in dealing with angry people is that you may also become angry. If you do, you lose. If you get angry, your anger and the complainer's anger will feed on each other. Then neither one of you will be susceptible to reason. So, no matter how angry the caller is, you must remain reasonable. Don't allow yourself to mirror the caller's anger. If you are friendly and upbeat, it is hard for the other person to stay angry.

The worst thing you can do is to argue with the client. If you react to angry people with a defensive attitude, you're just asking for abuse. When you argue, you have created a destructive game with you and the client on opposite sides. It becomes "you against me"—a game that at least one of you must lose. If you "win," you make the client look bad. That's not a great way to keep clients. On the other hand, if you "lose," you look bad; the client will think you're stupid; and nobody wants to buy from stupid people. So if you win, you lose, and if you lose, you lose. Being defensive is a can't-win situation. Your goal should be to create a constructive game with you and the client on the same side. Play "you and me against the problem"—a game you can both win.

When people feel that they are being attacked, they may react one of three ways, all of which are bad:

1. *Denial:* "I never said that," or "That's not what happened," or "You've got it all wrong."

2. *Blame:* "Those people in our typing department don't know how to spell," or "Our billing department is always sending out wrong statements to clients."

3. *Counterattack:* "It's really your fault," or "You've got it all wrong," (again) or "If you had only —, this wouldn't have happened."

These are bad responses because they invalidate other people. They make them wrong, or wrong for complaining to you. People don't like to be wrong.

This applies both to you and to the caller; no one likes to be invalidated. However, unlike the client, you can't afford to be emotional; you have to remain cool and in control. When someone feels invalidated, whether it's you or the caller, the anger usually intensifies. The old fight-or-flight syndrome makes the adrenaline pump through our veins like gasoline fuels a fire. So don't attack the caller, and don't take any perceived attack on you or the firm personally. Take the clients' anger professionally, not personally; they are usually mad in general, not mad at you specifically.

What do you do if callers do attack or insult you? *Ignore* it. They are speaking from their negative emotions and probably don't mean it. Even if they do mean it, so what? If you respond to the attack, it strengthens their feelings and tends to escalate the negative situation.

So respond helpfully, not defensively.

Practical Tips for controlling your emotions:

- Smile before you pick up the phone. It will come through in your voice tone. You will find that it is hard to tell someone "Go to Hell!" when you are smiling.

- Speak slowly.

- Take a deep breath whenever you feel yourself becoming angry or defensive.

- Remind yourself, "When others heat up, I must cool off."

I know that it is tough sometimes to let a slur, cheap shot, criticism, or thinly veiled insult pass, but do it. After you both have had a chance to think about it, you'll be glad you did. Remember that your goal is to handle the situation, not to aggravate it. *You* are the professional; it's your job to make things go right.

Your goal is to handle the problem at this first call. At this stage, the caller is angry at the problem, not at you. At this stage, the anger is much easier to soothe. However, if you respond by invalidating the caller, he or she may then get angry with you personally.

You will know this unfortunate event has occurred if the caller stops talking about the problem and starts talking about you. This is the stage at which the caller may insult you personally or use profanity. If you blow it here, the caller may threaten to take some action such as filing a lawsuit, calling the Better Business Bureau, or filing an ethics complaint with your licensing board.

Obviously, you never want to let a complaint get beyond the first stage—being angry with the problem.

You are probably dealing with the client over the phone, so be very careful with your tone of voice. Never, never, never be sarcastic or say anything that might be interpreted as sarcasm. Think of a client who is angry, antagonistic, or hostile as an overheated steam boiler. If you bang the boiler about and subject it to additional stress, it's likely to worsen and maybe even explode. Instead, allow it to vent its steam, and it returns to normal. People vent their steam by communicating. So they must have someone to communicate to. Listening is crucial for handling unreasonable people.

Never interrupt angry people; they are not open to reason when they are angry; their boilers are still overheated. If the client is angry, do not interrupt for clarification even if the tirade seems to make no sense;

angry people frequently make no sense. Just letting them talk will allow them to vent some anger, raise their emotional tone level, and recover some of their ability to reason. After they vent their anger, you can get clarification. But don't try to communicate to angry people: They literally will not hear you.

However, don't just remain silent. Occasionally say "uh-huh" or "I see" so that they will know that you are listening. Agree with them when you can. Encourage them to get all their feelings out into the open: "Is that right? . . . Go on. . . . Then what happened?"

Encourage them to tell you everything they're thinking and feeling. If complainers express negative generalities, such as, "You people are all just ripping off the public!" ask in a sympathetic voice, "What causes you to feel that way?" Watch your tone of voice; you really need to find out the answer, so ask in a voice tone that says "I really want to know." Remember, they will tell *someone*; you want it to be you, not their legislators.

Practical Tip:

Don't ask questions that start with "why." "Why" has a bit of blame or finger-pointing in it. Instead, use "what," as in "What do you think caused the —?" or "What effect did this have on your operation?"

Definitely, you should avoid either evaluating or invalidating what angry clients say. Don't analyze, interpret, or tell callers what to think about something. Just accept what they say as the truth *to them*. After all, it *is* their reality. You might take notes while they are talking. It helps you listen better, and, if the complainer is there in person, they can *see* you listening.

After hearing them out, summarize what you heard them say, including the emotion you received. "So you feel frustrated because we —," or "I can sense how you must feel about this." Here you are restating their feelings, as well as the facts. Though all feelings are facts the more angry the person feels, the more this is true; the very angry person is operating on a purely emotional level.

Thus, you cannot reason with people until you have handled their negative emotions. So don't try to handle these situations with logic—yet. You still have to handle the negative emotions. This may take a long time, but trying to handle the situation logically while people feel intensely angry will not help the situation and could hurt it because your motives may be suspect.

Some of you may find it distasteful to deal with people on an emotional level instead of a rational, logical level. You may think, "They should be reachable through clear reasoning no matter how angry they are." "If I handle their emotions, I'm just pandering to an irrational side of human nature." Or "anyone can be reached by reason at any time."

Unfortunately, despite what we may wish for, human beings simply are not *always* open to rational thought. Think of the times you have tried to reason with *homo sapiens* under the influence of heavy negative emotions. How successful were you? Try these suggestions for simply listening a few times, and compare the results with what happens when you respond with rational explanations. You'll find that letting people express their anger with you works, while appealing to their intellect at such times doesn't work.

Keep talking to them about the situation and their feelings about it until they have completely expressed their anger and have exhausted its source. Wait as long as you need to. From a purely selfish viewpoint, you're trying to protect your investment in this client; if you blow it, you've lost the client and created an enemy. And from a more humane viewpoint, the client will feel better and you'll feel better if you keep a positive relationship. The ideal result is for the client to laugh about it. When that happens, you know that the client's emotional tone is now high enough to address the complaint rationally.

If you have listened and restated for quite a while and the person doesn't seem to be able to exhaust the anger, the person's attention may still be stuck in the past. You may have to do something to get the person to come up to present time. One way to do this is to direct the client's attention to the current scene by asking the client to help you try to resolve the situation. Be sure to express your desire for the client's help in your voice, such as saying, "Mr. Jones, I want to help you, but I can't until you help me to understand exactly what the situation is. Will you help me? What can we do to work on this thing together?" Using the word "help" is usually beneficial, as is the word "together."

Eventually, the caller may even apologize for his or her attitude.

> **Key Point:** When a person is angry, first handle the anger, then handle the problem.

After you get the unreasonable person to be reasonable, you can handle the complaint in the regular fashion. However, what happens if the person just doesn't become reasonable, no matter how long and how patiently you listen?

WHAT ABOUT THE JERKS?

A few people, no matter what you do, won't become reasonable. On those rare occasions, you have to be philosophical and realize "Nobody bats 1.000." Occasionally, we all encounter a few real jerks.

> **Definition:** A *jerk* is someone who wants something for nothing, a person who takes advantage of your good nature to gain something at your expense, a person who is only happy when mad and who mistreats others for amusement, a deadbeat. (Cottle's dictionary)

Fortunately, 95 percent of your clients are not jerks. If they are being unreasonable, they think they have good reason, and you handle them as suggested in this chapter. The 5 percent or less who are jerks are a different case.

Jerks are not normal human beings; they are jerks. Don't accept jerks as clients. If you accidentally accept a client who turns out to be a jerk, fire the jerk. Your only concern in handling a complaint from a jerk is to protect yourself from legal liability and to try to get a little "damage control" on what the jerk will later say about you. However, no matter what you do, the jerk won't be satisfied (jerks are never satisfied) and will say bad things about you. Don't take it personally; jerks say bad things about everybody. Be philosophical about this, and don't lose any sleep over it. Chances are, a true jerk behaves like a jerk with those to whom he or she complains, so they'll pay little heed to the jerk's complaints.

Unfortunately, you usually don't know clients are jerks until you try several times to treat them as if they were normal human beings and they do not respond in kind.

A final thought: Be nice to everyone, even jerks. A friendly, open attitude sometimes works wonders, even with jerks.

Practical Tip:

Have all your frontline people read this chapter, and discuss it at a staff meeting. Soon, your firm will be turning complaints into increased client loyalty.

NOTES

1. Thomas J. Peters and Nancy Austin, *A Passion for Excellence*, New York: Warner Books, 1985, p. 96.
2. Peters and Austin, pp. 92–93.
3. Thomas J. Peters, *Thriving on Chaos*, New York: Alfred A. Knopf, 1987, p. 91.
4. A. Parasuraman, Valarie A. Zeithaml, and Leonard L. Berry, "A Conceptual Model of Service Quality and Its Implications for Future Research," *Journal of Marketing*, Vol. 49, Fall 1985, p. 46.
5. Robert Townsend, *Further Up The Organization*, New York: Harper & Row, 1988, p. 30.

18

Where Do I Go from Here?

Action without information is dangerous; but information without action is tragic.

David Cottle

Now you know the greatest single key to a successful professional practice: *high-quality client service*. And you know how to increase your clients' perceptions of the high quality of your service. What you do with that information is up to you.

I often tell my consulting clients about the doctor who was visited by a man complaining of feeling rundown; nothing specific was wrong, he just didn't feel up to par. After conducting a physical examination and asking the patient some searching questions about his habits, the doctor said: "My professional advice is to drink no more than two cocktails in any one day and to abstain at least four days each week. Further, you must quit smoking and lose 20 pounds. Finally, I want you to walk at least one mile each day at a brisk pace."

"You don't understand, Doc," said the patient. "I *like* to have a few drinks before dinner every night and then have a nightcap to help me sleep. And I get nervous when I don't have a cigarette in my hand. And I love to eat, and I hate to exercise. I don't want to change, I just want to feel better. Can't you give me some kind of pill?"

The doctor responded, "Like I said, if you want to feel better, drink less, quit smoking, lose 20 pounds, and walk a mile a day."

"No, no, no, Doc! You still don't understand. I have no intention of changing my lifestyle; I just a want a pill or something to give me more energy."

Whereupon the doctor said, "There is no magic pill. If you keep doing what you've been doing, you're going to keep feeling the way you've been feeling."

A lot of firms are like that patient when it comes to improving their service. If all they have to do is read a book, they'll do it. But when it comes to actually changing, they say, "Do I really have to listen to my clients? Do I really have to communicate better? Do I really have to show concern for their time? Do I really have to do all those things you recommend?" Zig Ziglar had the best answer when he said in a speech, "No! You can be mediocre without them!" There are no magic formulas; the information, tools, and methods I have given you require effort to make them work.

If you're not willing to *act* to improve your service, if you don't have the will to *change* for the better, then don't start talking about better service to your employees and clients. Just keep your fees low and hope that enough of your competitors are as mediocre as you are.

ACTION PLAN FOR IMPROVING SERVICE TO YOUR CLIENTS

But if you are committed and have the will and perseverance to put these ideas to the test, here is your action plan:

1. Treat Your Clients As If They Were Lifetime Partners.

Earlier, I compared the professional relationship to a marriage. For many professions, this lifetime viewpoint comes naturally. Family physicians, chiropractors, accountants, veterinarians, and corporate attorneys all expect to do repeat business with their patients and clients. But some professionals, such as architects, surgeons, or divorce lawyers might think their service is one that people buy only once in a lifetime. That may be true, but remember Lisa Ford's mother, whose surgeon sent her flowers. Referrals are word-of-mouth advertising—the best advertising there is.

Clients are an integral part of your practice. In fact, they are also part of your service delivery team because they always participate to some extent in rendering your service. How often, however, do we see clients on a firm's organization chart? This oversight creates an inward-looking practice, with attention focused on the organization and not on the client. So turn your organizational chart upside down, and list clients in a new box at the top. Just below them place your frontline people. Below them are your support staff. Management should be at the bottom. Learn to think of management itself as a service function whose job is to facilitate and support the front line in their mission of satisfying clients. Figure 17 shows this new view of your organization chart.

Treating clients as lifelong partners is easy to conceptualize and hard to execute. But the challenge facing the leadership of today's professional practices is to shift the firm's attention outward, away from the organization and toward the client. To paraphrase Karl Albrecht:[1] Management must continue to set direction, allocate resources, formulate strategy, make decisions, enforce priorities, and guide operations. But service-oriented management must also be supporter, helper, and enabler with the frontline people in their handling of their moments of truth.

2. Ask All Your Personnel for Service Improvement Ideas.

Ask your personnel these questions:

- What's the biggest or most frequent problem you face in delivering high-quality service?

- If you could wave a magic wand and make one change around here to improve our service, what would it be?

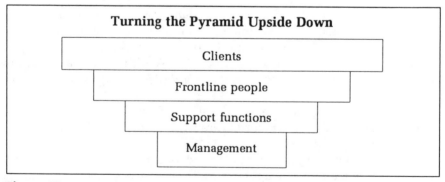

Figure 17

- Is there anything that we, as management, should stop doing that hinders your efforts to serve clients?

- Is there anything else that we, as management, should begin doing to enhance your results on behalf of clients?

Buy everyone in your firm a copy of this book. Then have a series of one-hour meetings each week to discuss ideas for improving external quality. Have a contest, complete with prizes or recognition for everyone who comes up with a workable idea for improving service. Consider sharing the profits from money-saving or money-making ideas with their creators.

3. If You Don't Have a Mission Statement, Adopt One.

Focus your firm's efforts on specific types of clients and types of service. Develop a clear picture of the kinds of clients you want and the types of services you want to render. That doesn't mean necessarily to turn down clients or services that don't match your model; just concentrate your marketing and service efforts on those clients you can best serve.

4. Carefully Recruit and Train Your Frontline People in the Fundamentals of High-Quality Client Service.

Training and developing your frontline people are nothing less than "product development." To a large extent, your front line *is* the product. If you want to realize the enormous financial benefits of leveraging your top partner talent with lower-level associates, they must be trained to deal directly and in depth with clients. Also, for the training to be meaningful, the employees must feel that they will directly benefit from it. That means that you must have an adequate reward system. Follow the advice in Chapter 15 to develop a high-quality cultural environment for your firm.

5. Always Be Patient, but Never Be Satisfied.

Service quality is not a destination; it is a journey. You will never be perfect, so settle for excellence. If your personnel can't perform as well as you would like, be philosophical and just make sure that they are better now than they were before. Then help them to get better still. Don't try to make people 100 percent better overnight. If they get just 1 percent better each week, think how far they will come in just a year!

THE BOTTOM LINE

Quality doesn't cost; it pays. Now you know how to increase client loyalty and how to create superior-quality service. You can use that knowledge either to charge fees that are 5 to 7 percent higher than average firms, or to grow much faster than average, possibly both if you are particularly good at marketing.

If you have lost clients that you shouldn't have, you can now improve your service and increase client retention. If you have clients who just didn't come back, you can call and reactivate some of them.

You can now win back referral sources who used to send you business but haven't for a long time. And you can increase referrals from existing clients.

The fees you charge and the amount of money you earn are determined by just four factors: (1) the demand for what you do, (2) your ability to do it, (3) the difficulty of replacing you, and (4) your ability to invest your time and other resources where they will yield the highest return.

This immediately gives you four different approaches to increasing billing rates:

1. Increase demand for your services.

2. Increase your firm's abilities to perform.

3. Make yourself irreplaceable to the client by distinguishing your firm from your competition.

4. Invest your resources in low-cost, high-yielding improvements in service quality.

The ideas I have given you will help in all four areas. Remember: Experience shows that if you don't implement at least some of these ideas within three days, you probably won't implement any of them. So start now! An enthusiastic client is the best business strategy of all.

NOTES

1. Karl Albrecht, *At America's Service*, Homewood, IL: Dow Jones-Irwin, 1988, pp. 107–108, 112.

19

Summary of Key Concepts

CHAPTER 1: WHY QUALITY PAYS BIG DIVIDENDS

The reason that clients change professionals is not fees but service. What clients want—and are willing to pay for—is high-quality service. High-quality service enables you to command higher fees.

> **Definition:** *Service excellence* is a level of service quality, compared to your competitors, that is high enough in the eyes of clients for you to charge higher fees, gain an unnaturally large market share, and/or enjoy a higher profit margin than your competitors.

A firm needs only a very small share of a very small market to be enormously successful.

High quality is more than a technical problem to be solved; it is a competitive opportunity.

CHAPTER 2: WHAT IS "HIGH-QUALITY" SERVICE?

Clients don't buy professional services; they buy solutions to problems and good feelings.

Client satisfaction equals client perceptions minus client expectations. Client perceptions and expectations are both subjective. Clients become enthusiastic only when service exceeds their expectations.

What clients receive is the service outcome or the internal quality of service. The manner in which the service is delivered is its external quality. In a professional practice, internal quality is created inside the firm, and firm personnel are the only people conscious of it. External quality is the face that the practice presents to the outside world.

Clients expect good internal quality and are not overly pleased when they get it. To get good marks with clients, a firm must manage not only its internal quality but also its external quality.

The key to ensuring high-quality service is to meet or exceed what clients expect. Therefore, determine exactly what problem the client wants you to solve and what "good feelings" means to the client.

Each client's expectations and perceptions reflect reality the way the client sees it; they may not reflect reality the way you see it.

To get clients to grade your services as high quality, make sure your client has realistic expectations of what you will be able to accomplish.

It is important with all new clients to determine why they left their old professional, if they had one, and what they expect of you. What, exactly, is the problem they want you to solve?

To turn "customers" into "cheerleaders," raise their satisfaction to a higher level.

CHAPTER 3: THE FIVE GRADES ON YOUR INVISIBLE REPORT CARD

Reliability is the ability to provide the promised service dependably and accurately. It includes timeliness and the client's perception of your competence.

Assurance is the client's feeling that her or his problems are in good hands.

Tangibles include the physical evidence and artifacts of your service, your facilities and equipment, and the appearance of your personnel.

Responsiveness concerns your willingness to help clients and to provide prompt service.

Empathy means that caring, individualized attention is provided to clients.

The most important client criterion for high-quality service (reliability) is the hardest for the client to evaluate. Clients usually evaluate service quality based on characteristics that they can personally experience and judge.

CHAPTER 4: "SMITH & JONES" VERSUS "ACE WIDGETS"—WHY PROFESSIONAL FIRMS ARE DIFFERENT

All products have aspects of the tangible and the intangible. The main difference between goods and services is the different proportion of tangibility, as compared to intangibility. Services differ from manufactured goods by the following characteristics:

- Services are intangible.

- Services require human interaction to some degree.

- Service quality control is very difficult.

Because of these differences, service quality is difficult for the consumer to evaluate, and consumer satisfaction is largely subjective.

Goods are produced first, then sold; services are sold first, then produced.

The value of a service varies from consumer to consumer, depending on the personal experiences, needs, and desires of each individual consumer.

Professional firms differ from other service firms in four key aspects: (1) Clients of professionals are at greater risk than the purchasers of nonprofessional services or products. (2) Professional services are customized to individual needs of the client. (3) Clients cannot judge the internal quality of professional services. (4) Professional relationships can continue for decades, even generations.

The customer relationship of manufacturers and retailers, especially of consumer goods manufacturers and retailers, is relatively simple. The marketing function serves as a screen between the company and the customer.

Professionals do not have such a simple relationship with their clients. Because services are simultaneously produced and consumed, production and consumption are mixed up with each other, as well as with marketing. The marketing function of professional practices cannot be separated from the production function.

The production of services includes all activities necessary to satisfy the client's requirements. Consumption of services begins when the client first encounters your practice and continues throughout the relationship.

Traditional marketing can sell clients once. Only interactive marketing can get them to buy again.

Definition: A *moment of truth* is any event in which a person encounters some aspect of your firm and gets an impression of the quality of your service.

Moments of truth are almost never neutral. They are either positive or negative to the client. Professionals interact with clients through three kinds of moments of truth: (1) office environment and other tangible representations of the service; (2) client-contact personnel; and (3) the clients themselves. These interactions are visible to the client.

The fourth way of interacting with the client is through the client's memories of past experiences with your firm.

Internal quality alone is not sufficient for client satisfaction. External quality is more important than internal quality to clients, so long as internal quality is adequate. External quality is especially important when clients are incapable of evaluating internal quality.

CHAPTER 5: POSITIONING YOUR FIRM IN THE MARKETPLACE

Market positioning can create product differentiation when people otherwise see all firms as identical.

Definition: The *market position statement* is the message you want to communicate about your practice. It is the distinctive image your firm has in the minds of clients, prospects, referral sources, and competitors. Your market position is based both on *facts* about your firm and on public *perceptions* of those facts.

Definition: The *USP* (unique selling proposition) is the single most important characteristic that both distinguishes you from your competitors and is valuable to clients.

CHAPTER 6: WHAT DO PEOPLE *REALLY* THINK OF YOU?

Key Point—Perception Principle Number One: Others always perceive a firm differently from the way the firm perceives itself.

Key Point—Perception Principle Number Two: Others perceive a firm differently from the way the firm thinks it is perceived.

Key Point—Perception Principle Number Three: Different groups perceive the firm differently from one another.

The purpose of the feedback program is to get feedback regarding your firm's service to the client or regarding a referral source's perceptions of your firm.

The purpose of measuring client satisfaction is to get the clients' mental report card in writing.

CHAPTER 7: WHAT BUSINESS ARE YOU IN?

Every service has a life cycle. A firm cannot successfully render services in all phases of the life cycle; the cultural differences are too great. The life cycle of professional services can also become the life cycle of the firm. All the various cultural implications must be addressed for the firm to remain viable.

Be client centered rather than resource centered because your client is a moving target.

To find what your business is, ask, "Who is your client? What does your client buy? What do your clients value? What do clients look for when they buy your services?"

Don't let your practice run by accident; manage it with purpose.

The *mission statement* is a client-centered and action-oriented statement of how you provide benefits to your clients. The mission statement describes the value that you offer your clients.

CHAPTER 8: HOW TO STAND ABOVE THE CROWD

Three facts to remember: (1) Reality is what you can perceive clearly. (2) People cannot clearly perceive the differences in your generic product. (3) People respond only to differences. This means that marketing power shifts from promoting a generic service to highlighting the ways in which prospects can perceive differences between firms.

You cannot achieve uniqueness in your basic, generic service. External quality is much easier and cheaper to improve than internal quality.

> **Key Point—Perception Principle Number Four:** People perceive that your performance in nonbusiness settings is an indication of your performance in your profession.

> **Key Point—Perception Principle Number Five:** People also perceive that your performance in one area of your business is representative of your performance in *all other* areas of your business.

CHAPTER 9: HOW TO PROJECT A HIGH-QUALITY IMAGE

> **Definition:** *Image* is a likeness or imitation of a person or thing, a mental picture or conception.

Clothes help make the sale. Tangibles include

- Your ambassadors—A good brochure or proposal won't get you any clients, but a bad one can put you out of the running.

- Your souvenirs—Clients pay special attention to the souvenirs as clues to your service quality.

After the appearance of your reception area, the next most powerful image prospects will get of your firm is how they are greeted and treated when they enter your offices.

CHAPTER 10: BEWARE THE SIX CAUSES OF SERVICE PROBLEMS

1. Inseparable production and consumption of service

2. Inadequate service to "intermediate customers"

3. Communication shortfalls

4. Statistics-oriented view of clients

5. Short-run view of the business

6. Service proliferation and complexity

CHAPTER 11: HOW TO MANAGE YOUR "MOMENTS OF TRUTH"

Traditional marketing gets the client in the door the first time; interactive marketing—relationship management—keeps them coming back again and again.

Managing moments of truth to enhance the client relationship is more important to preserve and enhance the intangible asset known as "goodwill" than is the management of tangible assets.

CHAPTER 12: HOW TO MANAGE CLIENT EXPECTATIONS AND PERCEPTIONS

Consider two aspects of each client's needs: service outcome and operating style. The first rule for happy clients: Give them what they want.

In planning each performance of a service, obtain an understanding with the client as to your responsibilities and the client's responsibilities.

To manage client expectations: (1) Avoid the promotional temptation to overpromise. (2) Learn to spot extremist clients in advance. (3) Don't oversell the service outcome. (4) Scale down the client's expectations. (5) Introduce the idea of multiple factors. Emphasize that you can *influence* events, but you cannot *control* them. (6) Educate the client and the client's family and other advisors. (7) Stay in touch with the client.

Manage the tangibles to shape client opinions during and after your performance of the service.

CHAPTER 13: THE KEY TO MOTIVATION

We cannot motivate other people. All we can do is to create a climate where they can thrive.

The opposite of job satisfaction is not job dissatisfaction but, rather, *no* job satisfaction; similarly, the opposite of job dissatisfaction is not job satisfaction, but *no* job *dis*satisfaction.

The most important satisfiers are achievement, recognition, pleasure from or interest in the work itself, and responsibility.

CHAPTER 14: MANAGE THE PEOPLE

All the *real* assets of a professional firm go home every night. It is the *people* who produce the results; technology only makes the people more productive.

Your receptionist, or whoever answers the telephone, is your "front door" to the world. If you get nothing else from this book, get this: Your receptionist (and your telephone operator and secretary if you have separate positions) are your most important salespersons. Never put a brand new person on the front desk without thoroughly training the person.

Executives should spend more time managing people and making people decisions than on anything else.

Anyone who is not given information cannot assume responsibility. However, anyone who *is* given information cannot avoid assuming it. Making everybody part of the strategic information stream makes everybody feel emotional ownership of the firm.

The number one motivator of people is feedback on the results of their efforts.

Coaching involves an investment of management time for the good of both the firm and the "coachee." Coaching is a mild teaching experience, as distinguished from criticism or a reprimand, which have negative emotional reactions. Coaching has no element of blame. If assistants feel bad when you coach them, you are doing something wrong.

If you are in the habit of overwhelming or intimidating your personnel (or your clients), they will look for another job (or another professional).

CHAPTER 15: HOW TO DEVELOP A HIGH-QUALITY CULTURE IN YOUR FIRM

Establish high quality standards. Hire personnel with the capacity to meet those standards. Train people to meet high quality standards.

Check to see that they *are* meeting those standards. Reward them when they are successful.

A partner's high income is derived from the firm's ability to leverage its partners' skills with the efforts of lower-salaried personnel.

CHAPTER 16: STAY IN TOUCH

Regularly communicate to clients what you are doing for them. Make your invisible, intangible services as visible as possible. Tangibilize your service.

Observe your clients as you are serving them and watch the good, bad, and mixed indicators of how well you are satisfying them with your services.

CHAPTER 17: HOW TO TURN COMPLAINTS INTO INCREASED CLIENT LOYALTY

A complaint is an opportunity to make the client a lifelong associate.

Most people are persuaded more by attitude than by logic. Complainers tend to adopt the same emotional attitude that you have.

Make sure your clients understand you are always *willing* to help them, even when you are unable. Five rules should guide your handling of client complaints:

1. Listen sympathetically to the complaint. The number one thing complainers want is to tell someone about the source of their complaint. And they will.

2. Show understanding and concern.

3. Mutually agree on a solution.

4. Follow through.

5. Follow up.

Also, ask yourself, (1) "What would have prevented this problem?" (2) "What changes should I make in our operations to ensure that this doesn't happen to someone else?"

In handling an unreasonable person, you have two assignments: (1) Handle the client's emotions, and (2) Solve the problem. You cannot reason with an angry person.

CHAPTER 18: WHERE DO I GO FROM HERE?

Information without action is worthless. Act on the information you've learned from this book. Start now.

1. Treat your clients as if they were lifetime partners.

2. Ask your personnel for service improvement ideas.

3. Adopt a mission statement.

4. Recruit and train your frontline people in the fundamentals of high-quality client service.

5. Always be patient, but never be satisfied.

Implement at least some of these ideas within three days.

AFTERWORD
Giving Credit Where Credit Is Due

I have been privileged to be a professional and a consultant for more than 20 years. During that time I have been an insatiable reader, student, seminar participant, and listener. I have been exposed to ideas at almost every turn:

- Professional literature of accountants, lawyers, engineers, consultants, physicians, etc. is rich with good ideas and I have read as many as I could.

- I am also an avid reader of general business books and magazines.

- I have attended countless seminars on everything from setting fees, to real estate investing, to strategic planning, to personal selling skills.

- I have taken voluminous notes, both written and mental, and I have quite a collection of books, articles, manuals, magazines, monographs, and outlines.

- I have also consulted with, learned from, argued with, and watched in action some of the top professionals in dozens of cities and towns in the United States, Canada, Australia, Hong Kong, England, Denmark, Jamaica, Switzerland, and other countries.

- And I practiced as a CPA for 12 years myself.

I have personally experimented with many different techniques in strategic planning, sales, marketing, recruiting, counseling, and the other subjects covered in this book.

I believe it was Ralph Waldo Emerson who said, "Everyone knows more than I do about something; in that, I can learn from him." That is certainly true for me.

This wide-ranging practical education presents a common problem to authors: Sometimes I can't remember the source of an idea. As Zig Zagler says, I have known some of the ideas in this book for so long that I consider them my own. In fact, many of my best ideas were probably swiped from someone else. I have followed Tom Peters' advice from *Thriving on Chaos* and copied, adapted, and enhanced ideas from the best!

To the extent that I remember or have a record of the sources I have given credit to the inspiration for my ideas. I have tried to be fair to the many fine minds that have enriched my storehouse of knowledge, and have cross-pollinated my thoughts. However, it is inevitable that I will get some credits wrong, or that I will not give credit where it is due. For this I apologize.

Index